"In my 36 years as a prosthetist, I have met many amputees. There are few who have the ability to deal with their tragedy in such a dignified way as Loretta. She is a shining example to us all."

~ Bob Watts
Prosthetist & Managing Director
Dorset Orthopaedic Company Ltd.

"…a book that reminds us that life is worth living, and even in the darkest moments there are glimpses of God and of a purpose for us all."

~ Tessa Watts
Director
Dorset Orthopaedic Company Ltd.

"I think anyone who enjoys inspirational books will find this book appealing. Loretta helped me by listening and offering advice when I was undergoing my own challenges after a surgical accident led me to have my left leg amputated below the knee last fall. She knew just what to say, told me of her own experiences, and told me how she had overcome her medical trauma and was now a happy, whole person. It was what I needed to hear!"

~ Kathryn Crawford
Aunt of supermodel Cindy Crawford

As a co-author, "Dan Brannan brings such compassion to the telling of Loretta's story because, as a person with type one diabetes he, too, faces the very real possibility of limb amputation. Thank you … for telling Loretta's story of tragedy turned to triumph. And thank you, Loretta for your courage, strength, determination and inspiration."

~ Rawnie Berry
Metro East Manager
American Diabetes Association

"Vicki Bennington and her co-author Daniel Brannan really bring alive Loretta's extraordinary journey from the most insignificant of household injuries to losing parts of all of her limbs—and then fighting her way back to what would be "normal" …. at a time when anyone paying attention to the news feels a little mutilated, *A Life in Parts* has a much-needed message of healing."

~ Chris King
Editor, Writer, Producer

"This book's reach is not only for those struggling with disabilities, but with anyone who has ever felt like life is not worth living ... the message is uplifting without the usual tactics to squeeze out the tears from the reader."

~ Adrienne's Reviews, Goodreads Reviewer

"I read it in one day's round-trip commute—not just because it is fairly short, but because it's a gripping read of the medical-crisis-and-recovery personal story genre ... Loretta seems well positioned as an expert for the generations of U.S. veterans who have and will come home missing limbs. Then there's the increasing crisis of bacterial infections like MRSA—all in all, there should be a large audience to identify with this book."

~ Christine Frank, Goodreads Reviewer

A Life
in Parts

A true story of an idyllic life, a devastating loss,
and one woman's resolve to rise above it

by

Vicki Bennington

and

Daniel Brannan

Stonebrook Publishing
Saint Louis, Missouri

A STONEBROOK PUBLISHING BOOK

Edited by Nancy L. Baumann

All photos used by permission, and are courtesy of the following:
Vicki Bennington
Wally Goebel
Sir Paul McCartney
Heather Mills
Dick Snyder Photography
The Telegraph, Alton, Illinois

Cover design by Jane Colvin
Interior design by Kristina Blank Makansi

Library of Congress Control Number: 2012939608
ISBN: 978-0-9830800-2-2
eBook ISBN: 978-0-9830800-3-9

www.stonebrookpublishing.net

PRINTED IN THE UNITED STATES OF AMERICA
10   9   8   7   6   5   4   3   2   1

A Life
in Parts

A true story of an idyllic life, a devastating loss,
and one woman's resolve to rise above it

Tom~
A pleasure to meet
you !!
God is good
    All the time!
        love, Loretta

Table of Contents

If you didn't know my story,
you wouldn't know my loss.

~ Loretta Goebel

Foreword

I had been an amputee for many years when I met Loretta.

My office was first contacted by a member of her local church, who explained that Loretta had lost her limbs. Out of their deep love for this valued and cared-for member of their community, her family and friends were searching for advice about how to help Loretta move forward after such a serious tragedy and trauma had befallen her.

I insisted on meeting Loretta in person, and I am so pleased that I had the pleasure of getting to know her and her family. Experience has shown me that it is so important to meet fellow amputees after their life has been turned upside down, because they are thrown into the deep end of an experience that only those who have gone through a similar trauma can truly understand.

If I was able to help Loretta and her family come to terms with her tragedy and to move forward to tackle her new life with a renewed zest and vitality, then that fills me with a warmth inside and a sense of pride. I know that Loretta now inspires others every day with her positivity, and that she will continue to help, motivate, and inspire other amputees by her wonderful example. Love is reciprocal, and planting that seed of love has borne a wonderful flower in Loretta.

Loretta is a beautiful and feminine woman. The limbs that she wore when I first met her were not. When her stalwart husband, Wally, first wheeled Loretta into my hotel room during her recovery, I could completely relate to her shock, her trauma, and her disdain for those clunky, heavy limbs she had been given. As a model myself before my accident, I totally understood and related to Loretta's need to preserve her femininity.

I was very pleased to explain to Loretta that her current prostheses were not the only option she had, and that so much more was now possible. I then  proceeded to lift up my trouser leg and show her my own prosthetic. Loretta was very excited by my limb, and now aware of her own possibilities, we decided then and there that the type of leg I wore was the way forward for Loretta. I explained that the swelling in her limb would need to reduce first, and then she could be fitted with a beautiful cosmetic limb in Dorset County, England.

We spoke often after our first meeting, and eventually Loretta was ready to come to the U.K. for her fitting. Loretta was truly invigorated by her new limbs. It was a joy to see the light shine in her eyes and to see her wonderful family's sadness begin to dissipate, because the amputee is not the only one who suffers. Family members also experience trauma when a loved one endures such difficulties, and they are often forgotten when the amputee is rehabilitating. I felt such warmth from their love for Loretta, and it was wonderful to see their spirits lifted, as well.

Love is a reciprocal action. My counseling rule has always been thus: that if I do my best to help a fellow amputee, then when they are fully recovered, they will go on to help others in the best way they can. Loretta has gone on to inspire so many in her community, and now with this book, her amazing story will go on to inspire many thousands more. You are a beautiful flower Loretta, and it was a pleasure to meet you and your family. May you plant many seeds of love with your inspirational story.

Heather Mills
June 2012

PART ONE

Coming Apart

Never deny a diagnosis, but do deny the negative verdict that may go with it.

~ Norman Cousins

Wally wheeled her through the doors and shouted, "I need help! Help us, please!"

It was 7:00 P.M. and the ER was bustling. A baby screamed for its mother; the automatic doors whooshed open every few seconds, ushering in frigid blasts of air. Its icy tentacles wrapped around her frail body that already convulsed with shivers. She slumped forward in the wheelchair, pale and weak.

He rapped his knuckles on the counter. "My wife is really sick here," he called out, a controlled firmness in his voice.

The receptionist barely looked up. "It will be a little while," she said. "We'll call you when it's your turn."

"Listen to me!" he insisted. "We were here last night. They sent us home, but now she's much worse." Here last night ... now much worse ... those words sounded the alarm bell, and the attendant snapped to attention.

"We need a team to the front desk, stat!" she shouted. The nurses swarmed, and they clamped on a blood pressure cuff and inserted a thermometer in her ear. Her body temperature didn't even register. Hypothermia had set in.

"BP 40 over 20!" one nurse shouted. It was well below the 120 over 80 norm for a healthy female—and far below the danger level. The nurse removed the cuff from Loretta's arm and saw the sharp, red line that started at her thumb, shot up her arm, and disappeared into her armpit. She locked eyes with the patient, then looked away.

Chapter 1

It was an unlikely day for an invasion.

Loretta Goebel sensed no threat as she carefully wrapped Christmas presents in the basement of her northern Illinois home. It was December 11, 2001, just two weeks before Christmas. Her two children were at school, and her husband, an air traffic controller, was at work. As she was curling the final ribbon on a gift for her mother, the doorbell rang. She dropped her scissors and rushed to answer it, and as she darted around the corner, she banged her right hand on the banister. "Ouch!" she shouted, grimacing in pain, but she shook it off and ran up the stairs.

It was Norm, the UPS man, delivering more Christmas packages. Loretta knew she would be seeing a lot of Norm in the coming days. They had developed an easy friendship, and she always gave him a drink of some sort during summer deliveries, and they often stopped to chat for a few minutes.

"Something wrong with your hand?" Norm asked when he saw her rubbing it.

"No, it's fine. I just hit it when I ran up the stairs. Let me sign for this and you can be on your way. It's too cold and you're too busy this time of year to hang around with me," she said with a smile. "Merry Christmas, Norm."

Surrounded by farm ground, the Goebels' house was nestled in a collection of oak and hickory trees near the city of Sycamore, about sixty miles west of

Chicago. They built the house in 1992, when their son Mitch, now nine, was just a baby. Two years later, their daughter, Alyssa, was born. Gradually, their home took shape and was transformed into exactly what they had planned—a backdrop for a life that could be shared with their families and a long list of close friends and neighbors.

Some people are born to entertain. They love the little details that turn normal hospitality into a Martha Stewart experience, and Loretta was one of them. She started decorating for Christmas as early as possible, usually by the first of November. The minute they switched their porch lights off on Halloween night, she packed up all the pumpkin decorations, and the next day, the kitchen tree went up. They put their main tree in the family room, but Loretta couldn't see it from the kitchen, which is where she spent so much of her time during the holidays. Not willing to miss out on the festive atmosphere, she bought another tree for the kitchen and, from there, it snowballed.

By the time she was finished, they had eleven Christmas trees. A bit over-the-top, she admitted, but when her family came home or her friends came over, she wanted them to be saturated with the holiday spirit. The kitchen tree was loaded with gingerbread figures, the living room tree sparkled in ivory and gold, and in the family room, the blue spruce glistened in iridescent silver. Mitch and Alyssa each had a tree in their bedroom, and Wally and Loretta had two: a Victorian tree in the master room and a smaller one in the adjoining sitting room. Scented candles burned throughout the house, and the subtle aroma of pine and cinnamon, mingled with the smell of baking cookies and hot cider, often wafted through their home.

Making their home beautiful was Loretta's joy, but she was passionate about nurturing the family within. Hearty food was on their table every night—hot soups, crisp salads and vegetables, seasoned pot roast or chicken, potatoes and rice. During the holidays, she played Christmas music in the background, traditional hymns or contemporary carols, just loud enough to hear, but not so loud that it intruded on their dinner conversations.

The Goebels spent most of their free time as a family. It was rare for Loretta and Wally to hire a sitter because when they went out for dinner, they took Mitch and Alyssa with them. They wanted to teach their children from an early age how to conduct themselves in public. And yet, Wally and Loretta carved out time for each other after the kids were in bed. They planned "date nights" in the playroom, drank White Zinfandel and watched movies, talked and laughed, and connected. When they snuggled in bed, she loved the feel of his breath, his warm touch. Every night Loretta fell asleep with her hand tucked under Wally's hip.

When morning came, it was all about the kids. Loretta fixed breakfast, then waited outside with them, going over their flash cards or spelling words up to the minute they got on the bus. After they left, she stayed outside if the weather was warm and worked in the yard or jumped on the trampoline for exercise, blasting Shania Twain or Meatloaf from the speakers and jumping for an hour or more. As she often said, any stress in her life was purely self-inflicted, and it was usually because she had overcommitted to her church or friends.

The children's Christmas program at her church was one such commitment, and just an hour before she hit her hand, Loretta sat in the kitchen with her friend, Lisa Feuerbach. They were directing the program, which was just five days away. The two sipped coffee and finalized the remaining details while Lisa's baby slept nearby in her car seat. Several other parents had also volunteered to help, and Wally was cast as the narrator. Since Mitch and Alyssa were both in the choir, Loretta's entire family was involved.

Lisa left around eleven, and Loretta tidied up the kitchen, fixed some lunch, and went down to the basement to wrap presents—which was what she was doing when Norm rang the doorbell.

The afternoon tumbled into evening, and after they ate dinner, Loretta dropped Alyssa off at her dance class. On the way back home, her head started to feel thick and heavy. Something wasn't right, but she couldn't quite pinpoint the problem.

She got home and had just enough time to phone Wally's sister, Diane, in Michigan before heading back out to pick up Alyssa. Wally's whole family—his parents and sisters, plus their spouses and kids—were coming for Christmas. All in all, there would be seven guests, plus the four of them. Loretta treated her guests like royalty, particularly if they were family, not because she was pretentious, but because that was her way of honoring them. She put mints and freshly cut flowers in every bedroom and had plenty of towels, Q-tips, shampoos, and perfumed soaps in the bathrooms. When they arrived, there were baskets of treats in each of their rooms, special snacks that had been purchased and assembled with one thing in mind: their comfort.

And then there were the meals. She not only planned the formal Christmas dinner, she charted out their entire visit and made lists of everything she needed for every meal they would share, lists that not only included the food she would serve, but what candles would burn and what music she'd play. She purchased special napkins and tablecloths that fit the theme for each dinner, and her homemade candies and cookies were already sealed in Tupperware containers and stored out in the garage to keep cool. But she was nowhere near being finished. In fact, Loretta was behind schedule.

Before she bought all the groceries, she thought she should check in with Wally's sister to be sure that everyone would like what she had planned. She phoned Diane to go over the menus, but they were just a few minutes into the conversation when Loretta interrupted her. She was suddenly nauseous and felt drained, wrung-out like a dishrag. Unbearable aches seized her muscles, and her head banged inside her skull. She felt like she'd been flung into a brick wall.

"I'm sorry," she told Diane. "I have to go. I feel like I've been run over by a Mack truck."

Chapter 2

Loretta hung up without saying goodbye and tried to quell her waves of nausea. Deep aches settled in her muscles, and by the time she left to pick up Alyssa, she felt like an ice carving. She cranked the heat up as high as it would go and willed herself to get there and back as quickly as possible.

"Hi Mom," Alyssa said as she hopped in the car.

Loretta tried to smile, but she was frozen, paralyzed. Her fingers were stiff, and an icy rod had replaced her spine.

"What's wrong?" Alyssa asked. "Why is it so hot in here?"

"I must be getting sick," she answered. "It just hit me after dinner. I feel awful, and I'm freezing to death."

Back home, Loretta made a cup of hot tea and headed upstairs to put on her flannel pajamas, but even that required all her energy. Her feet were heavy, like she was wearing lead boots, and the staircase seemed an impossible climb. When she finally reached the top, she had to sit down to catch her breath. She struggled to get in bed, but was certain she'd be fine tomorrow.

But Loretta was not fine the next morning. She had spiked a fever, couldn't eat, and was crippled by lethargy. Even so, she dragged herself downstairs to take care of the kids. Being sick was no excuse to neglect her responsibilities, no matter how she felt. She fixed their breakfast and made their lunches—but she wore her winter coat the whole time.

"Why are you wearing your coat in the house?" Mitch asked. "It's weird."

"Well, for some reason I'm cold. I'm sure I'll warm up if I keep moving around," she said. "Hurry up and finish, so I can tidy up the kitchen."

Mitch looked at his sister and shrugged. They finished eating and went out to catch the bus, but this time Loretta didn't go out with them. She watched through the window as they boarded, then plopped down at the kitchen table. She pulled her coat tighter, sipped her coffee, and tried to absorb the sunlight that poured through the window, hoping the bright rays would make her feel better.

The rest of the day was mostly a blur, but she did call Lisa to talk about the Christmas program.

"What do you mean you're sick?" Lisa asked. "You were just sick at Thanksgiving! You seemed fine yesterday. You have to get better—I need you!" she said emphatically.

"I know. I'm so sorry," Loretta said. "I'm sure I'll be better tomorrow."

When Wally got home from work that evening, he was a bit alarmed. Loretta was rarely ill, and if she was, she bounced right back, usually within the day. "I think you should call the doctor first thing in the morning," he told her.

Thursday afternoon, she sat in the exam room. "Sounds like the flu," the doctor said.

"I just had the flu over Thanksgiving," Loretta said. "Do you think it's the same thing?"

"No, that was a stomach virus. This looks like the flu," he said, "which is also a virus, so it won't help to prescribe anything. Go home and go to bed, and be sure to drink plenty of fluids. You'll be fine in a couple of days."

On Friday, Loretta was still sick. Her undone tasks and unshopped-for items multiplied in her mind, and the pressure of everything she needed to do for the holidays distressed her. Friday was Wally's day off, and he offered to help by running her errands and working off some items on her to-do list. Loretta agreed, although she would normally never burden him with her responsibilities. He came back home with the bar stools from Target that she wanted for extra seating and some other purchases, but she couldn't even get up and go downstairs to see them.

Lisa called the next day. "Just checkin' in to go over a couple of last-minute details for the program tomorrow," she said. "Are you feeling better?"

"Maybe a little … but no, not really," Loretta answered. "I still can't get out of bed. I'm really sorry, but I don't think I can make it to rehearsal tonight."

Lisa was stunned. "This isn't right, Loretta. You've been sick since

Wednesday. I think you should go to the emergency room."

"I can't. If I did that, Wally would miss the rehearsal," she said.

"We love Wally," Lisa said, "but we'll get someone to fill in for him." Despite Lisa's insistence, Loretta couldn't be swayed. She would not take Wally away from his responsibility.

When he got to the church, he caught up with Lisa. "She might be doing a little better than she was yesterday," he said, "but it's hard to say. Sometimes she seems better, but then she feels sick again."

But Loretta was not getting better. At three in the morning on Sunday, December 16—six days after she hit her hand—she was jolted awake by a severe pain in her right arm. It started at the base of her thumb where she had smacked it on the banister, shot all the way up to her armpit, then descended down her right side. Her arm throbbed, and it felt like her heart might beat right out of it. Thinking she had slept on it wrong and that her arm was asleep, she squeezed and kneaded it, trying to wake it up, but deep down she feared it was more than that.

Loretta didn't normally give into pain. Even during childbirth, she preferred to deliver her babies without medication. Having a baby had been painful, but tolerable; this pain was deep and merciless.

Wally had been sleeping on the daybed in the playroom so he wouldn't catch her bug, and she dragged herself down the hall to get his help. It was slow going and exhausting. Her legs felt like dead weights, like she was dragging them through a dream. She clung to the wall for support and inched her way to her husband.

When she got to the playroom, she collapsed in the rocking chair to wait out the pain, playing devil's advocate with herself as she weighed her choices. Did she really want to tear her family out of bed on a frigid night to go to the hospital? She didn't have to make that decision. Wally heard the chair creak and was startled awake. He looked at the clock. Its soft glow spread across the room—3:10 A.M.

"What are you doing?" he asked.

"My arm is killing me," she said. "I think I need to go to the emergency room."

Wally snapped into action. In their eleven years of marriage, Loretta rarely complained. She would normally never suggest such a thing. He grabbed

Alyssa and Mitch from their beds and pulled their coats on over their pajamas.

"What's wrong? Where are we going?" they asked, warm with sleep.

"Mom still doesn't feel well, so we're going to the hospital to let the doctor check her out," he told them.

When Loretta didn't pause to brush her hair or put on any makeup, Wally's chest tightened. She never left the house, not even to run to the store, without getting ready. He piled everyone in the car, and they sped to the hospital.

In the exam room, the attendants removed her pajama top and noticed the thin, red line that ran up the length of her arm. The doctor ran some tests and diagnosed her with an infection: acute lymphangitis. He put her on an intravenous antibiotic and some strong pain medication, then sent her home a few hours later with a prescription for an oral antibiotic. She was back in her own bed by six o'clock. Wally made breakfast for the kids, then ran to the pharmacy to fill her prescriptions.

Thanks to the medicine, Loretta didn't feel much pain, but she was still miserable, and she spent another day in bed. Whenever she ate, she immediately threw up. She tossed and turned, unable to get comfortable. Her sleep came in fits and starts. When she was awake, she was consumed with worry about the Christmas program and their family plans, convinced that her lists had now grown lists.

That afternoon she phoned her friend, Mary Phelan, in Ohio and told her about their early morning trip to the hospital. Loretta and Mary were old friends and had met when their daughters, then three years old, were in the same dance class. The class was in nearby Genoa, Illinois, which was, to Loretta's dismay, a parallel-parking-only town. Loretta was hopeless at parallel parking, unable to back in and park the conventional way. She could only manage it if she found two spots back-to-back that she could pull into front first. Every time she took Alyssa to dance, she prayed that she would find a double space. She later joked with the other moms about her parking handicap, and Mary overheard her. That was all the invitation that Mary needed. She wanted to get to know this woman who said parallel-parking prayers.

Soon they were carpooling to dance every week, and the two became close friends, "glamour moms," as they nicknamed themselves, but not because they were snobbish or conceited—they were nothing like that. Mary and Loretta were both fashionable and feminine, and they always tried to look their best.

In fact, Loretta didn't even go out to get the mail if her hair and makeup weren't done. She liked to be fixed up and presentable at all times, and Mary was the same way. Mary had moved to Cincinnati with her family a little over a year ago, but their friendship was still strong, and they talked on the phone nearly every day.

"I have something called acute lymphangitis," Loretta told her.

"That doesn't sound good," Mary said. "Maybe they should have kept you at the hospital."

"I'm sure I'll be fine," Loretta said. "I just need to sleep it off and let the antibiotic do its job."

Mary wasn't convinced, and she did a little research of her own. She didn't like what she found. Lymphangitis is an infection of the lymphatic vessels and is often a complication of bacterial infections. Frequently termed *blood poisoning*, it can be serious. When bacteria spreads out of control through the lymphatic system, it can invade the lymph nodes—where the infection-fighting cells reside—and weaken the immune system. At the acute stage, it can be fatal.

Alarmed, Mary called back to tell Loretta what she had learned, but Mitch answered the phone and said that his dad was busy taking care of his mom. She didn't get to talk to either one of them, so she left a message for them to call back.

The Christmas program was just hours away when Lisa phoned again. Loretta, full of guilt and regret, said she couldn't make it. "Don't worry about it. I'll get some other mothers to fill in," Lisa said, "but in the meantime, I want you to call your doctor back."

"Not yet," Loretta said, "the medicine hasn't had enough time to work."

"Loretta! You've been on the antibiotic long enough that you should be improving by now! Please, call your doctor!"

"I have to give it more time," Loretta whispered into the phone, too weak to speak any louder. "I still have a fever, but I'm not in as much pain. I just want to sleep. I'm so … tired."

But time was running out, not only on the Christmas program, but on her very life.

Chapter 3

Loretta wasn't the only one who was tired; the rest of the family was exhausted from their early morning trip to the emergency room. They each took an afternoon nap, and then it was time to get ready for the Christmas program. Wally helped the kids get dressed while Loretta lay in bed.

She was sad that she wouldn't even see, much less be a part of, the program that she helped produce, but she didn't dare show her disappointment in front of her children. They stood by her bed, all dressed up in their Christmas attire. Alyssa had long dark hair, big brown eyes, and her mother's captivating smile. She looked so sweet in her blue velvet dress, white tights, and black patent shoes. Alyssa was the more outgoing of the two and would be the exuberant singer tonight. Mitch, in his dark suit, tie, and white shirt, looked older than his nine years. He was the image of his father with blue eyes and light brown hair, a little tall for his age. Mitch was quite an athlete, but was a bit more reserved than his mother and sister.

Tears sprung to Loretta's eyes, but she blinked them back and said, "You guys look amazing, and I know you'll be awesome. Have fun tonight."

They kissed her goodbye, but before they left, Wally paused. "Let me put on your Celine Dion CD, so it's not so quiet in here," he said. He plugged in the lights on the bedroom tree, flush with Victorian roses that matched the wallpaper in their room. From her bed, Loretta could see the glow from the sitting room tree that cast a soft light over the ceiling and walls.

"This is lovely, Wally," she said groggily. "Thank you."

Earlier that day, Wally had called Loretta's mother, Wanda, and told her that Loretta was still sick. "Would you mind giving her a call around six tonight, just to check on her? She'll be home alone, and I think a phone call would do her good." Wanda instantly agreed.

On the way to church, Wally couldn't stop thinking about Loretta, and before he even left their driveway, he knew he couldn't stay at the program, that he couldn't leave her at home alone, not in this condition. She had been taking the antibiotic since early that morning, but she still hadn't improved, not even a little bit. Her eyes, usually bright, were cloudy and flat, and they could barely focus. Something was terribly wrong; he could feel it in his gut. He took the kids inside, then handed his script to another dad who had helped at the rehearsals.

"I have to go," Wally said, "I'm taking Loretta back to the emergency room." Another parent volunteered to take care of Mitch and Alyssa after the program, and Wally bolted out the door.

When he walked back in their bedroom, he froze.

If he hadn't been in his own house, he wouldn't have recognized his wife. She lay still as stone and appeared much smaller than she really was, as if she had shrunk down and been swallowed by the pillow. Her skin was translucent, like fragile bone china. She barely rustled the sheets when she heard Wally come in.

"Why are you back?" she whispered.

Wally fought his alarm and steadied his voice. "We're going back to the hospital," he said gently. He was terrified by Loretta's condition, but he didn't want his fear to frighten her.

"I can't go anywhere without a bath," Loretta said weakly, "and I need fresh pajamas."

Wally thought about objecting, but he knew he couldn't change her mind, so he took her hand and helped her out of bed. She opened her nightstand drawer and pulled out clean pajamas. Clutching them to her side, she shuffled to the bathroom, but before she reached the tub, she pitched forward and collapsed, crumpled on the cold tile floor. Wally rushed in and lifted her up, then helped her down the stairs. It was too cold to take her outside, so he sat her at the kitchen table and went out to warm up the truck. When he came back, the phone was ringing.

"Hello?" he barked.

"Wally? Why aren't you at the program?" Wanda asked. She had expected her daughter to answer. "What's going on?"

"I came back for Loretta. We're going back to the ER," he said. "I'll call you when I know what's going on."

Even though a heavy fog was moving in, Wally shot off like he was driving the Indy 500. "Slow down," Loretta cried out. "Slow down." Her head bobbed from side to side as the truck bounced along. She was too weak to hold it steady.

They pulled up under the emergency canopy, and Wally grabbed a wheelchair. He burst through the doors, shouting, "I need help! Help us, please!"

It was seven o'clock and the ER was bustling. It was nothing like the quiet scene at three that morning. The staff, busy attending other patients or processing paperwork, didn't pay much attention to Wally. They either didn't notice his urgent cries or didn't have time to care. A baby screamed for its mother. The doors whooshed open every few minutes, and the frigid air blasted in, wrapping its icy tentacles around Loretta, who was already wracked by shivers.

Wally rapped his knuckles on the counter. "My wife is really sick here," he said, a controlled firmness in his voice. Loretta slumped forward in the wheelchair, pale and weak.

The receptionist barely looked up. "It'll be a little while," she said. "We'll call you when it's your turn."

Loretta was not the type to push ahead, didn't ever force herself on anyone. But she knew she didn't have time to wait. "Please help me!" she shouted in a strained whisper, "I cannot wait!" The woman looked up.

"Listen to me!" Wally said. "I brought her in last night. They sent us home, but now she's much worse." *Here last night ... now much worse ...* those words sounded alarm bells, and the attendant snapped to attention.

"We need a team to the front desk, stat!" she shouted behind her, rallying several nurses to Loretta's side. They wheeled her back to the patient area—an antiseptic ward where privacy curtains separated one exam room from another. They clamped on a blood pressure cuff and put a thermometer in her ear. Her body temperature didn't even register. Hypothermia had set in.

"BP 40 over 20!" one nurse shouted. It was well below the 120 over 80 norm for a healthy female—and far below the danger level. The nurse removed the cuff and noticed Loretta's arm. A sharp, red line traced a trail from her thumb, ran up her arm, and got lost in her armpit.

"Can you help him?" Loretta whispered. "Can't you help that little boy?" she asked.

The nurse bent over to meet her eyes. "Help who, honey? What little boy?" she asked.

"That little boy. I can hear him. He can't breathe. Shouldn't you go help him?"

From the other side of the curtain, the nurse heard the labored wheezing and gasping of a child, an asthma patient under attack. "He'll be fine," the nurse answered. "Don't worry; we'll take care of both of you."

The attending physician examined Loretta, then formed a huddle in the hall with several other doctors and nurses, deep in discussion. He gestured for Wally to join them.

"She's in critical condition," he said, "but we don't have the resources to treat her here. We need to transport her to a larger hospital in Rockford. We would normally airlift her by Medivac, but we can't do that now. The fog is too thick, and all helicopters are grounded."

As an air traffic controller, Wally knew the perils of flying in fog. He looked out the window; visibility was near zero. He wouldn't have allowed Loretta to fly, even if the hospital had arranged it. He wouldn't let any aircraft take off in this soup. She would have to go by ambulance—when they could locate one.

"She's not stable," the doctor told Wally as he signed Loretta's care over to the transport team. "She may not survive the ride," he said. "I hate to be blunt, but it's the truth."

The ambulance bustled with nurses and technicians who loaded Loretta's gurney head first, facing backward. Though barely conscious, Loretta was aware of what was happening, and an unpleasant childhood memory floated to the surface.

She was on vacation with her parents and sisters. It was the days when seat belts weren't required, and she and her sister, Laura, had turned completely around and were "playing the piano" on the back of their seat. They stared out the back window and made music in their minds while their car rode the waves of the Ozark hills, mounting and cresting, cresting and falling, up and down, up and down. Loretta could feel it now, could feel the nausea rising and crowding her throat, just like it did that day. Laura had screamed for their daddy to stop the car, and they piled out and threw up on the side of the road, right in front of someone's house. A woman ran out from the kitchen, her hair and apron blowing back in the breeze, and she handed each girl a lemon slice to suck until their nausea finally disappeared. Loretta didn't want to ride backwards in the ambulance. She was afraid she'd throw up and make a big mess that someone else would have to clean up.

Wally reached up to climb in with her, but was stopped at the door. "I'm sorry, there's no room for you," the technician said. "You'll have to follow in your own vehicle."

"But the doctor said she might not make it. I need to ride with my wife!"

He looked at Wally's frantic eyes and said, "I'm sorry, sir, but we only have room for our team. We'll meet you at the hospital."

Dec 16, 2001 - my arm (right) hurts so bad I wake-up Wally at 3am to take me to the emergency room. We snatch the Kids from their beds and head to town.

After an IV of Antibiotics and some Rx's to fill we come back home around 6am.

The Christmas program is this evening and my heart hurts that I will miss it. The kids are dressed to go and look so cute. Wally takes the kids made Arrangements to get them home as we are going back to the hospital. I about pass out. I am not well.

Chapter 4

Loretta met Wally, a muscular former marine with a prominent mustache, when he was twenty-seven and new to the Chicago area. Originally from Michigan, Wally was an air traffic controller at the Chicago Air Route Traffic Control Center. His job was to control en-route air traffic, and his facility served the Chicago and Milwaukee metropolitan areas. Loretta was twenty-four at the time, and she worked as the lead teller at the local bank. When Wally came in to open an account, all the new account reps were busy, so even though Loretta was a teller, she assisted him. As they finished up their business, Wally handed her his phone number, but Loretta just laughed. She already had a drawer full of numbers that she'd never called.

Every couple of days, Wally pulled through the drive-through lane, and the tellers would say, "Loretta, the man with the funny sunglasses is out there—you know, the ones with the yellowish lenses." She would go out to chat with him, and then later he'd call her and say, "Where's the grocery store? Where's this? Where's that?"

Finally, she accepted his invitation to dinner.

He took her to a nice Italian restaurant and ordered a bottle of White Zinfandel which, over time, became "their drink." Always the gentleman, Wally opened doors for her, took her arm, and pulled out her chair before she sat down. When they walked on the street, he was always on the outside, and he never walked two steps in front or two steps behind her. They talked about everything and matched each other mind for mind, surprised by their similar interests and passions.

A few weeks later, when Loretta got off work at the bank, she stopped by the apartment complex where she was working part-time, which in a roundabout way, helped move their relationship forward. It was a simple job. Loretta showed the model units to prospective renters, and in exchange for that, she got to use the swimming pool. The frigid winter was melting into spring, and when she got to the property, she noticed a piece of fiberglass that had fallen on the patio. She picked it up, but slipped on what she swears was the last patch of ice in the state of Illinois, fell to her knees, and was greeted by the loud crack of snapping bones. Her ankle had broken in two places.

No one else was around. Loretta pushed through the pain, crawled inside to find a phone, and called a friend to take her to the hospital, where they surgically inserted pins and plates to hold her ankle together. She was discharged wearing a bright pink cast, with strict instructions not to drive until it came off.

That was a problem. A new Hyatt hotel was opening in nearby Lisle, Illinois, and they were in the process of hiring a full staff. Loretta had always wanted to be part of the hospitality industry and had applied for a position before she slipped on the ice. Now she had to find someone to drive her to the interview. She asked Wally if he would give her a ride, which he was more than willing to do, and he sat at the bar and waited for her while she snagged the job.

It was perfect for her. The hotel was a popular site for outside conventions and other meetings, and Loretta was in charge of those events. She met with the clients and worked with them on the setup, the audio/visual needs, and the food and beverage requirements. Her natural flair for entertaining was an asset, and the job helped refine that talent.

She'd been working there a few months when the manager of the Hyatt in Long Beach, California, hosted a convention at her hotel. Loretta was in charge of the event. When it was over, the Long Beach manager called her boss and said he wanted Loretta to work for him as his Private Line Manager. He thought she was the perfect person to work with the executives of their core clientele, and he told her that if she committed to the job for two years, she could transfer to any Hyatt she wanted, anywhere in the world—an attractive offer to a woman of twenty-five. Before she agreed, Loretta wanted to see the work environment for herself, and they arranged a preliminary visit. She called

Wally and said, "Guess where I'm going?"

She was picked up at the airport and whisked off to the hotel in Long Beach. They said, "Here's your office, here's your name tag, here's your secretary, and here's your itinerary. Tonight we're having a pool side reception for you to meet some of your clients. Here's the Rolodex of the people who will be here. And tomorrow, someone from human resources will take you out to help you find an apartment."

The muscles in her neck seized. Find an apartment tomorrow? Her mind raced and she stammered, not sure how to respond, not sure that she should say anything at all. This was supposed to be an exploratory trip, but they clearly assumed she was committed. She felt trapped, like she'd already been roped in. Loretta fretted in silence the rest of the weekend, yet her sunny disposition and positive persona confirmed to her colleagues that she was perfect for the job.

On the flight back to Chicago, the man sitting next to her probably thought she'd been to a funeral because she cried the entire time. Like clothes tumbling in a dryer, her thoughts cycled: *What am I going to do? I grew up in Shipman, Illinois, a town of only five hundred people. Do I even fit in this part of the country, a place that is foreign to me? The salary is more than I'm making now, but it's not enough to live on by myself. I'd have to find a roommate. And I have to be able to come home to visit because my parents will never come to California. Two years is a long time. And what about Wally?*

She went straight back to the Hyatt in Lisle, only to learn that someone had already been promoted to her position. She talked to her manager, described the trip, and said, "It may seem like a weekend in Long Beach wasn't enough time to make a decision, but I know in my heart that I can't commit for two years."

Wally picked her up after work that day. They hadn't had time during her busy weekend to talk, and he had wrestled for three days with the fact that he might lose her. He drove around for a few minutes then pulled over in the Dairy Queen parking lot. The air was thick with the unasked question. Finally, he turned to her.

"Did you make your decision?" he asked.

Loretta sat quiet, then a soft smile tugged at her mouth. "I'm not going," she said.

Then Wally—stoic, Marine Corps Wally—jumped out of the car and turned a cartwheel, right in the middle of the Dairy Queen parking lot.

From that point forward, Loretta and Wally were a couple, always on the same page, always in lockstep regarding what they liked and didn't like, about their hopes for the future, and their long-term goals. If they had a choice of five different ways to spend their time, they would, without fail, always choose the same thing. As it turned out, one of the other managers at the Hyatt in Lisle was transferred to a different location, and Loretta took that position, putting her career dilemma to rest.

They were engaged for over a year, and during that time, they had a lot of work to do. Wally owned a house in DeKalb, Illinois, which was where they planned to live, but it was steeped in testosterone from the furniture to the painting to the decor. He'd already remodeled the bathroom and the kitchen, but the other areas needed an immediate facelift, and it desperately needed Loretta's lighter touch.

They were an industrious couple and were determined to do the work themselves, always eager to learn the necessary skills. They knew what they wanted and did not compromise on quality, always pushing for a professional result. After a major accomplishment, Loretta would call her mom and say, "We just hung this huge piece of crown molding in the living room. We measured twice and cut once, nailed it up, and the wedding is still on!"

They honeymooned in Hawaii, thanks to some incredible job perks that allowed them to travel. As one of the managers, Loretta could go to any Hyatt hotel and stay for three nights with no charge. And since Wally was an air traffic controller, he could fly for free on what was called a "familiarization flight." He was technically supposed to sit in the cockpit and observe the pilots, but Loretta would have none of that. She insisted he sit back in the cabin with her. They island-hopped for twelve days, staying three nights on this island, three on another, and on their way home they stopped in Scottsdale, Arizona, for a few days. Even after their honeymoon, they took advantage of the perks and made it a point to travel every six months or so.

But all that changed when Mitch was born. A homemaker and nurturer at heart, Loretta enthusiastically stepped aside as chief event planner to become a stay-at-home mom. When Mitch was a few months old, they decided to build a new house in Sycamore, Illinois, so they put the DeKalb house on the market. They were lucky. The house sold within a week, but that meant they had to move to an apartment until the new house was ready.

Loretta couldn't stand that apartment, but they couldn't move into their new house until it passed inspection, which meant, among other things, that the ceramic tile in the kitchen and bathrooms had to be finished. But the inspector didn't care anything about the floors in the other rooms.

"Just get it to pass inspection, and we'll move in," Loretta pressed the builder. And they did. They hauled their furniture and all their belongings into their house that was naked from the inside out. There was no trim around the just-caulked windows, planks of plywood served as the living room floor, the stairs awaited their on-order carpet, and they tacked bed sheets over the windows for privacy. The house seemed empty, but only to the untrained eye. Its true substance was within them, inside Loretta and Wally, who were confirmed in their goals and the vision that would take them there—one vision, one goal, one path, one step at a time.

Chapter 5

Wally knew he couldn't keep pace with the ambulance once it got going, so he left the parking lot while they were starting Loretta's IV. He wanted to get down the road as far as possible before it caught up to him. *Please God, please save her,* he prayed. *I can't lose her. The kids can't lose her. Please help us!* The fog was opaque, a gray floating wall; he couldn't even see the hood of his truck. To make it worse, he was unfamiliar with the road to the hospital and was terrified that Loretta would be dead when he got there.

A siren approached from behind. Muffled by the fog, it screamed like a wailing tomcat. He looked in his rear view mirror, but could see nothing. Red lights flashed past, then were swallowed by the night, as brief as a shooting star. He stuck his head out the window to try to track the siren, but the sound had also disappeared, sucked into the black hole of fog.

Wally followed the road, but when he entered the city, he panicked. He didn't know where he was and didn't know where to go. His wife was dying, and he couldn't get to her. Or was she already dead? *God, help me!* He couldn't waste precious time to stop for directions—he had to find the hospital on his own. When he stopped at the next intersection, the fog pulled back like an opening curtain.

The hospital was right in front of him.

Loretta was already inside in one of the examination rooms. "Is she alive? Is she alive?" Wally called out. "Yes, she's in here," the nurse answered. He rushed into the room and was relieved to see that she actually looked a little better. The IV fluids had plumped up her cheeks and returned a bit of color to her face.

The doctor burst in, the spitting image of Peter Falk from the old TV series, *Columbo*. Except for its color, his white coat, wrinkled and sagging, looked just like the detective's rumpled old trench coat. He plucked out a pen, and as he was firing off questions, he gave himself a thorough pat-down, searching all his pockets for a pad of paper. He finally grabbed a napkin off the counter and started scribbling.

He even sounded like the TV detective. "So tell me, what has happened to you in the last few days? And I see you went to the ER this morning. What happened there? Have you eaten? Have you had a fever today?" He peppered them with questions until the nurse came in to draw blood, then Loretta was whisked away for a CT scan.

While she was gone, Wally took a moment to call their neighbor who was watching Mitch and Alyssa. "Loretta's in critical condition, and I have no idea when I'll be able to come home," he said. "Would you mind getting them on the bus tomorrow with your kids?" Assured that they were settled, he turned his full attention to his wife and the results of her scan.

"This is pretty serious," the doctor told them. "Loretta, you have a severe infection. We have to pump you full of fluids to protect your major organs, and that won't be pretty. It will make you swell up like a beach ball."

She grimaced, and Wally squeezed her hand.

"The medicine will make you breathe really hard and really fast, and you won't like it. You may have to be on a ventilator for awhile."

The doctor administered Levophed (norepinephrine) in order to raise her blood pressure, which was still dangerously low. The drug would cause the bulk of her blood to be directed to her major organs, which would preserve their function while she battled the infection.

He pulled Wally out to the hall to give him further details. "Levophed can be a lifesaver because it raises the blood pressure," he said, "and once it is elevated, the antibiotics will stimulate her immune system and attack the infection.

"But I need to warn you. Levophed is not risk-free. It has serious side effects. Most of her blood will be directed to her major organs, which means that her arms and legs could be severely deprived, particularly the fingers and toes. The lack of blood flow can cause the limbs to die. In short, if she lives through this, she could lose some—or even all—of her extremities.

"The medical community has a saying about Levophed," he continued. "It's *Levophed or leave them dead.*"

Wally shook his head. "I don't understand. What does that mean?"

"Levophed is a drug of last resort," he explained. "She may ultimately lose her limbs, but if we don't give her this, your wife is going to die."

Wally stared at the floor, silent. He looked up and met the doctor's eyes, tears tracking down his cheeks. "Take her hands, take her feet, I don't care. Please … just save my wife."

"We'll do everything we can," the doctor replied. "But even with the Levophed, she still might not make it."

Almost immediately, Loretta's breath came hard and fast, puffing and chugging like a steam locomotive—whew-whoo, whew-whoo, whew-whoo, whew-whoo—and it never slowed down. She was groggy, but still conscious, and her eyes, wide with fear, darted around the room in panic. Bags and bags of IV fluids were pumped into her veins and, as promised, she swelled up like a balloon.

She needed another CT scan, and as they wheeled her out, Wally called to her, "Wait, Loretta! I need you to fight," he pleaded. "Fight, Loretta, this is serious."

She couldn't speak; her breath was fast and furious, and her heart pounded like a hammer. But she had understood Wally and wanted him to know that, yes, she was a fighter, and she would fight this. As they wheeled her into the corridor, she made a weak fist and raised her right thumb … *thumbs up, Wally.*

It was the last thing she remembered for a very long time.

Loretta slipped into unconsciousness during the CT scan. She was put on a ventilator and entered a drug-induced coma. The ICU had its own team of nurses, and she was assigned to Nurse Steve, an unlikely-looking nurse, in Wally's opinion. Steve had several tattoos, had a ponytail that cascaded down his muscle-bound back, and both of his ears were pierced. Wally took one look at Steve and thought, *Who is this?* He wasn't sure how he felt about Loretta being under his care, but his hesitation was short-lived. Steve rendered expert care, and he was a quick thinker who had earned a reputation for swift actions.

Without even looking at the chart, Nurse Steve immediately recognized the signs of acute lymphangitis. "See this red line on her arm? It's a textbook sign of lymphangitis," he said, "which is a complication of a bacterial infection. The infection is caused when bacteria enters the body through a cut or a scratch, or maybe even an insect bite. Has she had surgery lately? Sometimes bacteria can enter through a surgical wound or other skin injury."

Loretta hadn't had surgery, and Wally said that he couldn't think of anything that could have caused the infection. "But wait," he said. "She told me she hit her hand when she ran up the stairs the other day, and after that, her arm really hurt. That's why we went to the hospital in the first place."

Steve inspected Loretta's hands. Though she was meticulous about all other aspects of her appearance, her hands didn't fit her overall image. They were constantly in water, especially during the holidays with all the cooking, cleaning, candy making, and general preparations. She had even scrubbed her kitchen grout with bleach and a toothbrush a few days earlier. In addition, the frigid Illinois winters made it impossible to keep her hands soft and smooth. Simply stated, Loretta had dry, cracked winter hands.

Much later, her doctor would theorize that her cracked skin had been the perfect point of entry for group A streptococcus bacteria, which normally resides on human skin and other surfaces without causing harm. When she hit her hand on the banister, that blunt trauma propelled the bacteria into her bloodstream, where it invaded and went wild.

The doctor returned to the room and asked Wally to step out in the hall with him, away from Loretta's earshot. "Your wife's gone into toxic shock. There are pus pockets on her side that are a sign of a deep infection trying to surface. When toxic shock settles in, it sends clumps of toxins and tons of micro emboli throughout the body that can cause organ failure," the doctor explained. He looked Wally in the eye, "It's time to call her family. It's going to be touch and go, and anyone who needs to be here should come immediately."

Charles and Wanda Keck, Loretta's parents, hadn't heard from Wally in several hours and Wanda pounced on the phone when it rang. "Wally?" she answered.

"You need to get up here right away," he said. "She's in serious trouble."

"Oh my gosh!" Wanda cried. "Charles! Charles come here!" she yelled for her husband, then spoke back into the phone, "We hadn't heard from you, so we were just on our way. We'll be there in a few hours."

Charles drove while Wanda prayed out loud. "I'm scared," she said. "God, please take care of Loretta, and help her get better. She needs to be there for those little kids."

When they got to the hospital, they did not recognize their daughter. The ventilator squeezed out its rhythm, forcing breath in and out of her lungs, whooshing and gasping its pathetic tone. She'd been pumped full of drugs and fluids, which added seventy pounds to her slender, 125-pound frame.

"Oh, Loretta," Wanda cried. She went to her bedside, but didn't—couldn't—bring herself to touch her own daughter for fear of hurting her. She glanced at Charles, who was clearly in shock, visibly trembling as he leaned down and gave his daughter a soft kiss on the cheek. Speechless, her parents clasped hands and listened to the ventilator's pump-whoosh, pump-whoosh, pump-whoosh.

Wanda phoned her other daughters and told them about Loretta's deteriorating condition. Linda was the oldest, followed by Loretta, Laura, and then Lola. She and Charles had thought long and hard when they named the girls. They wanted their names to start with the same letter because, for them, it was a distinct way of connecting them as sisters.

"It's bad," she told Linda. "They've done everything they can. All we can do now is wait and pray. Keep praying."

"What do you mean, Mom? She has the flu! I thought she just had the flu," Linda said, choking back tears. "Do they know what it is?"

"They're calling it toxic shock. It's an infection that got into her entire system," her mother said.

"We're coming. We're all coming. Be strong, Mom," Linda said.

At midnight on Monday, Linda and her husband arrived at Loretta and Wally's house. It was too late to go to the hospital, but Wanda and Charles were inside waiting for them, and they filled them in on the details.

"She's on life support, and they're giving her strong antibiotics to fight the infection," Wanda told Linda. "She's all swollen up, so be prepared. You won't even recognize her."

"Swollen? Why is she swollen?" Linda asked.

"They gave her extra fluids to protect her organs from the infection," Wanda said. "I don't understand it all, but that's what they said. They're trying to save her life."

Wally drove back home on Tuesday morning to shower and change clothes, and he asked Linda to ride back to the hospital with him, so he could talk to her alone.

"Loretta and I have never talked about this, but do you think she would want to be buried here in Sycamore or back home?" he said.

"What … why are you asking me this?" Linda cried.

"If she doesn't turn the corner soon, it may come to that," he said. He wiped his eyes with the heel of his hand, but it didn't do any good, he couldn't push back the tears. His face turned red, and he swallowed quickly, trying to compose himself, so he could finish the conversation. "If … if she dies, will you and your sisters plan her funeral?"

Linda dropped her head in her hands and groaned. Her chest felt like it was being crushed. This was *Loretta* they were talking about, her little sister, the sunniest, funniest person she knew, the center of their family and her heart. *Her funeral? Loretta's FUNERAL?*

She reached out and rested her hand on Wally's shoulder, sensing the weight of what those shoulders carried right now. Her hand slid down and squeezed his. "Of course, we will. We will, if it comes to that," she said.

On Tuesday afternoon, Laura and Lola arrived, and their father prepared them to see their sister. "She doesn't look like herself," Charles said, "so try to stay calm. Getting upset doesn't help the situation, and it sure won't help Loretta."

Laura took one look at her sister and collapsed, falling into a nearby chair. "This can't be Loretta," she said. She gasped for air, and Loretta's nurse knelt in front of her and said, "Breathe, honey. Just breathe normally." Charles shot Laura a look that said, "Stay strong."

But this was hard for Laura, who was closest in age to Loretta. Linda was already nine years old when Loretta and Laura came in quick succession, with Lola three years behind. Just fifteen months younger than Loretta, many of Laura's childhood memories were of the two of them. Whether they were concocting a new perfume from a mixture of bathroom products or decorating their driveway by painting the gravel, the two were inseparable, and they were always up for an adventure.

One winter day, they decided to take a shortcut on their way to see their grandparents, who lived just beyond a neighboring field. They normally circumvented the deep, wide pond that lay in their path, but the rippling water had transformed into a plate of ice that glistened in the sun. It looked sturdy enough, so why not give it a try? They stepped out, holding hands. About a third of the way across, the ice splintered and emitted a loud *crack! pop!* as it protested their weight. Their hearts froze. Every step made a spider web of the surface. It was too late to turn back and too dangerous to run, so the little girls clung to each other and took baby steps until they reached the other side. They never walked on a frozen pond again.

Laura pulled herself together and went to her bedside. She and Lola leaned over and put their arms around their sister.

"Don't worry Loretta, you're going to get better," Lola said. "I'll take care of Mitch and Alyssa and everything at the house, so you can just rest and get well."

"We're all here for you," Laura added. "God is watching over you and the kids. We all love you."

Though the whole family was clearly distressed, they never said anything about Loretta's condition or her prognosis when they were with her. They didn't want her to hear anything negative, but wanted to fuel her with the hope and strength she needed to fight for her life.

Laura pulled a silver cross from her purse, engraved with the words *God Loves You.* "Do you have some tape I could use?" she asked the nurse, then tore a piece from the roll and taped the cross to Loretta's right shoulder, directly on her skin.

"Can we leave this on her? I mean all the time," she asked the nurse.

"I don't see why not," she answered. "If she goes to surgery, we'll have to cover it with more surgical tape, but that shouldn't be a problem. I'll try to make sure it stays on."

It was getting late, and Loretta's sisters went back to the house to fix dinner and look after the kids, but Wanda and Charles weren't ready to leave, not quite yet. They were visibly shaken, but Wanda knew Loretta had one major thing going for her—she was a fighter.

She turned to Charles. "She will fight. I know she will," she said quietly as their daughter clung to the underside of life.

Chapter 6

When they finally left the ICU, Wanda and Charles drove back to the house in Sycamore. Wally stayed at the hospital.

Charles pulled in the driveway and turned off the car. "Why don't you go on inside," he said. "I need some time to think."

Wanda complied; her anguish was just as deep, and even though it was bitterly cold outside, she didn't voice her concern about him sitting out in the car in the sub-freezing temperature. Like Charles, she was weary and needed some time alone to collect her thoughts.

The living room was empty. The rest of the family had either gathered in the kitchen or gone to bed. Some of the children lay on pallets with their parents wherever they could find a spot, though few slept. Wanda sank down on the living room couch and prayed that God would spare her child. *A ninety percent chance that she'll die!* she thought. *Lord, how can that be?*

Loretta had always been the picture of health. She was a stickler about nutrition, and watched her weight with a practiced eye. She worked out every day and rode bikes and played sports in the backyard with the kids. Loretta was vibrant—*healthy*—and Wanda couldn't grasp this turn of events. *Please, God, let her survive,* she pleaded.

Wanda was afraid, but her faith was strong. She was a lifelong member of the Lutheran church and had raised their girls in a strong, Christian home. The family attended church every week, then went home to a hot and hearty Sunday dinner, a tradition that Loretta continued in her own family.

After a few moments of quiet, Wanda's exhaustion fell upon her. She forced herself off the sofa and climbed upstairs, where she would sleep in the playroom with one of her granddaughters. She crawled into the daybed and hugged the child close, and they folded their hands together and prayed.

"Lord, we know there is nothing we can do but turn Loretta over to you," Wanda prayed out loud. "We know that she will either stay here on earth, or you will take her to heaven. We hope you will leave her with us and heal her." The bed was cramped, Wanda's mind was reeling, and sleep did not come easy that night.

Meanwhile, Charles still sat out in the driveway, numb. Was this really happening? He couldn't grasp that his Loretta, his little "Queke" as he called her, the girl he'd taught to ride a bike, who sat on his lap and watched *Gunsmoke* and *Red Skeleton*, might die. He had always taken care of his family, had always done everything to make things right, but he could do nothing for her now. Nothing.

God, please bring her back to us, he prayed. *Heal her. Take it all away.* Though Charles was a solid rock around his family, alone in the car, the dam inside him finally burst. His head dropped to the steering wheel, and like a rain-swollen gully, the grief poured out of him. He sobbed to the point of exhaustion, repeating over and over, *Please, please save her!*

Who knows how long Charles sat out there? The piercing cold finally invaded the car and bit through his clothes; he was sure his toes had frozen. Sapped of his strength, he opened the door, climbed out of the car, and dragged himself up the front walk, his head so low that his chin grazed his chest.

Wally, too, needed sleep, but he didn't dare go home. He wanted to be near Loretta, so he rented a dorm-type room in a section of the hospital reserved for the patients' families. His head was a tornado, a whirlwind of faces and facts that he needed to sort out. There was the ICU staff of doctors and nurses who buzzed around Loretta, and all the medications he thought he understood when they had been explained to him, but now he couldn't remember their purpose or their perils. In addition, the infectious disease team kept popping in, trying to isolate the exact cause of her infection. It had been one crisis after another, and each phase brought another set of unfamiliar faces, all critical to her survival.

I can't keep track of it all, Wally thought, *I've got to write this stuff down.* He started a journal, which was nothing more than a spiral notebook where he could take notes when each doctor stopped by, changed or added to her medications, or reported her vital signs. It also served as a makeshift guest book, and almost every visitor wrote a message to Loretta and her family, or recorded the medical information if Wally was out of the room.

By now, Loretta's friend, Lisa, was beside herself. She hadn't slept for more than an hour or two at a time since Wally had bolted from the Christmas program two days before. She knew Loretta was seriously ill because Wally called her on Monday and said they had transferred her to a hospital in Rockford. "But what's happening now?" Lisa fretted. "A lot can happen in a day. Call me, Wally, call," she willed, and practically flew across the room when the phone rang.

"Hello? Wally?"

"It's bad, Lisa; really, really bad," he said. His voice wavered, then cracked, and Lisa sat still and listened to him sob. "She has toxic shock. She might need surgery to drain some of the infection, but even that might not save her. They don't know if she's going to survive.

"And then there's the kids. I have to get them to the doctor to get checked for strep, too. That's how this whole thing started," he added.

"Strep?" Lisa repeated. "I don't understand. What does strep have to do with anything?"

"Her tests showed that strep was the source of the infection. Apparently it often resides on our skin without causing any problems, and even if it gets in the bloodstream, the body normally fights it off. But Loretta's immune system didn't respond fast enough, and the infection spread to her lymph nodes and overpowered her immune system."

"But I thought you said she had toxic shock and she was having surgery for that?"

"She is," Wally answered, "Strep gives off a poisonous toxin that can build up and cause toxic shock syndrome. Since she couldn't fight off the strep, the toxins built up and the infection went wild."

"How can I help?" Lisa asked, wiping her own tears. "Can I take the kids to the doctor?"

"Thanks, but her sister is going to do that," said Wally. "Just pray for her."

"Of course I will, but that's not enough. I'll make some calls and start a prayer chain," she said. "Tell Loretta I love her."

Wally hung up and phoned Mary. He knew she would want an update, too. "Loretta may not make it, Mary. I thought you might want to come to say goodbye, just in case."

"We're on our way," she promised, so shocked she could hardly reply. She and her husband dropped everything in Ohio and headed to Rockford, where they joined the crowd that had already gathered at Loretta's bedside.

The hospital staff was extremely lenient. They knew Loretta's time could be short, so they allowed the family to set up camp in the ICU. Someone was always with her—and with Wally, too. Their family, friends, and pastor grouped around her bed, but Loretta was all hooked up, and no one could get close enough to embrace her. Tubes snaked across her body and connected her to all sorts of monitors and machinery, the ventilator pumped her breath in and out, and the IV continued its drip, drip, drip.

Despite the equipment that separated them, Lisa sensed Loretta telling her, "Thank God you're here, Lisa. Take out your Bible and start reading." So the visitors surrounded her bed and began to pray, each reading a passage from the Bible. There were no dry eyes that night.

On Tuesday evening, December 18, a full week after she struck her hand, Loretta's temperature—which at one time hadn't even registered on a thermometer—shot up to 104 degrees. Her heart raced at 130 beats per minute, a sign that her immune system was starting to fight the toxins, but her elevated temperature and accelerated heart rate stressed her fragile system.

By the next day, she had not improved. She was, in fact, getting worse. Her blood pressure plummeted, and even though she was receiving a massive dose of antibiotics, the infection continued to spread. She seemed to be in pain, so the doctor started her on morphine, and the nurse moved the IV to her leg where there was better circulation and a larger vein to accommodate the drugs. There were indications that her liver was shutting down. Further, the doctors were concerned about her lungs. "We'll have to do a tracheotomy if her breathing gets worse," they told Wally.

Just when they thought Loretta couldn't get any worse, she did. The toxic shock escalated to septic shock, riddling her entire body with infection.

Gangrene could soon follow. The doctors decided they couldn't wait any longer. They had to drain some of the infection, so they took her to surgery and lanced the abscesses that had erupted on her right side, making three separate incisions, each three inches long. The surgeon left the wounds open and packed them with gauze to absorb the accumulating pus and discharge.

Afterward, the doctor found Wally in the waiting room and pulled him aside. "It doesn't look good," he said. "This may be her last night. You should probably prepare your kids for the worst." Then he spoke to everyone else. "We've done everything medically possible for her. We don't know if her brain has been affected, but every other organ is immersed in toxic strep."

No one spoke.

Then Lisa looked up. "Well, have you seen miracles?" she asked, as she met the doctor's eyes with firm confidence.

He nodded. "All doctors have seen miracles."

"Well, get ready," she continued. "You're about to see another one."

They stayed with Loretta and prayed throughout the evening, watching for the slightest sign of improvement. "Alyssa, Mitch, and Wally need you, Loretta," Lisa whispered in her ear. "You have to fight! Fight as hard as you can, so you can be here for them. Don't let go. We all need you." Immediately, Loretta's heart rate spiked.

"I think she can hear us," Lisa said. "Look what happened when I mentioned the kids' names!" Again, Lisa prayed specifically for Loretta's children, and her heart rate increased. They hoped it was a sign that her brain was still functioning, but there was no way to know.

As distressed as everyone else was, Wally's job was wrenching. He had to tell Mitch and Alyssa that their mother might die, possibly tonight. On the drive home, he rehearsed a number of ways to break the news to them in a serious but hopeful way, but nothing sounded right, nothing sounded true. He was about to break their hearts, and there was no way around it.

When he walked in the house, he found bodies scattered everywhere— nieces and nephews, brothers- and sisters-in-law, his own siblings—some even bedded down under the dining room table. Wally didn't disturb them. He snuck up the back staircase to look for his children and brought them into his bedroom. He still didn't know what to say.

Wally gazed at his son, only nine years old. He thought about how Mitch's life would change if he were stripped of his mother. Alyssa, just seven, was wearing a flannel nightgown and the hair bow her grandmother had hastily tied that morning. It looked limp and sad, unlike one Loretta would have tied. Who would fix Alyssa's hair now? Though he was determined to be strong in front of the kids, Wally couldn't help himself. Tears flooded his eyes when he saw his children on the bed, sitting side-by-side in a still and formal manner that betrayed their fear. They looked at him with wide, trusting eyes.

"What's wrong Dad?" Mitch asked.

Wally knelt down in front of them. "I have something to tell you," he said. "You know that Mom's been really sick, and we've been praying for her to get well. But she isn't getting better. She's getting worse. The doctor said she might not make it."

Mitch's jaw dropped, and Alyssa started to cry.

"What do you mean?" she asked.

Wally took a deep breath and forced the words out. "It means Mom might die."

"She can't die!" Mitch screamed. "Can't they give her more medicine?"

"They can't, Mitch. They're already giving her everything they can," Wally drew the children close, pulling them into his broad chest. "We don't know why she's so sick. But she's in God's hands, and we need to keep praying." He held them tight, and they cried and hugged each other even harder.

"We've always been a team, and no matter what happens, we will still be a team," Wally said. "Mom has always been the one to take care of us, but now she needs to know that we can take care of each other, no matter what, and that we'll get through this."

"I want my mom," Alyssa cried. "I want to see her!"

"I know you do, dumplin," he said. "We'll go to the hospital first thing in the morning. But I don't want you to feel scared when you see her. She doesn't look like herself right now because she's really, really sick. There's a machine that helps her breathe, and the medicine has changed the way she looks—she's all puffed up, and you may not recognize her. But she's still Mom. We'll go see her in the morning, and you can talk to her."

Wally lay down with his children, and together they prayed that Loretta would survive the night. Silently, individually, they hoped she would still be alive when they got there.

Chapter 7

No one slept much the night of December 19—eight days after Loretta hit her hand. While Wally talked to the kids, a heavy assignment weighed on Loretta's sisters. They needed to plan for Loretta's potential funeral. Laura was still at the hospital, but Linda and Lola thought they should start the discussion.

"I think she'd want to be buried closer to home, in Bunker Hill near Grandma and Grandpa," Linda said. Their grandparents were buried in a large cemetery not far from their home town, and it seemed like the likely resting place for other family members, too.

"And Uncle Charles is buried there, too," Lola added. "I'm sure she'd like to be near her godfather." She thought a couple of minutes more, and nodded. "Yeah. She'd want to be near where we grew up. What do you think she'd want to wear?" she asked Linda.

Linda suppressed a laugh. "Well if you asked her, she would probably say her fifth-grade cheerleader uniform." She smiled through her tears and thought about Loretta's vivacious personality and how she had always been a cheerleader, how even as an adult, she always urged others to be and do their best.

Lola took it a step further. "And how about her Homecoming crown? She would love that."

The truth was, they had no idea what Loretta would want. They had never discussed such a thing. And why would they? They were all young and healthy and thought they had plenty of time.

As they talked into the night, the doorbell rang numerous times, marking the delivery of hot, fresh food from their neighbors, their church family, and even from people who barely knew the Goebels, but had heard about their misfortune.

Though thoroughly depleted, Wally couldn't sleep. Doors opened and shut, feet tramped up the steps, toilets flushed, and he could hear muffled voices down the hall. Even if it had been stone-cold silent, his mind reeled, spinning fact with fear and morphing fear into fact. When he finally dozed off, his frantic dreams jolted him awake again. He lay in the dark, afraid that the phone might ring and praying that it wouldn't. Obediently, it sat silent. The hospital never called.

Wally got the kids up early the next morning and gave them a bowl of Fruit Loops before heading to the hospital. Mitch and Alyssa looked forward to seeing their mom, but Wally was agitated. He didn't know what to expect. Even if Loretta hadn't deteriorated during the night, whatever her current condition was, it would disturb and confuse the children. They hadn't seen her since they left for the Christmas program, and even though she was sick at the time, she still looked like their mom.

They parked near the entrance and, not one to wait, Mitch ran ahead and was first to enter her room. Wally was close behind with Alyssa in his arms. The pump and swoosh of the ventilator confirmed that she was still alive, but there was no way to prepare the children for what they saw. Their mother was all hooked up with tubes and wires, her eyes shut tight in artificial sleep. An antiseptic smell hung in the air and stung their noses. Alyssa buried her face deep in Wally's neck. Mitch hesitated for a moment, suddenly queasy, then marched over to her bed.

"Hi Mommy," he said. He rubbed her hand, careful not to disturb any wires.

Tentative at first, Alyssa joined her brother, and she stroked her mother's arm while Mitch described the scene at home and all the cousins who camped out there.

Loretta's eyes fluttered.

Wally turned to the nurse, a question on his face. "Wha ...?"

"She's actually doing a little better," the nurse said. "Her blood pressure is stable and her oxygen intake has increased. And her temperature's come down."

"Does that mean she's going to be okay, Dad?" Alyssa asked.

"Is she still going to die?" Mitch blurted, afraid of the answer but needing to know it anyway.

"This is just what we wanted to hear," Wally said. A smile cracked his worn face that had, for days, vacillated between stoic and sad. "She must be getting better!"

The tension broke. Mitch and Alyssa visibly relaxed, and they talked to their mom, telling her this and that, and when the doctor came in, they watched while he examined her. He confirmed it—the life and death crisis was over. "She's gained some control over the infection," he said, "and her vital signs have improved. We're giving her a sedative so she'll continue to sleep, which will help her body heal. We'll monitor her for a couple more days, and as we gradually decrease the medication, she will wake up. But remember, we still don't know what, if any, brain or organ damage she may have sustained. It's a wait-and-see situation."

Wally phoned the house to spread the good news. "We're out of the woods!" he proclaimed. "Loretta is on the mend." Within minutes, Charles and Wanda were in the car and on their way, thankful their prayers had been answered and eager to see their daughter.

In many hospitals, social workers are an integral part of the health care team, attentive to the needs of the patients, as well as their families. One such worker stopped by Loretta's room and asked Wally if she could spend some time with Mitch and Alyssa. "We're here to help if the kids are having trouble processing their mom's illness," she said. "Sometimes an outside person can detect underlying problems before the family even notices them. May I have your permission to talk with them?"

"Sure," Wally said. "It's fine with me, but only if they want to."

She took the children to a nearby cubicle for art therapy, and when they came back, she had a good report. "It's complicated," she said, "and they don't understand all the details, but they know their mom is very sick. I think they're handling the situation remarkably well."

The kids chattered and laughed for the first time in a long time, making jokes with their grandparents and acting their age, until they got tired and bored. It had already been a long day. They wanted to play with their cousins, so Wanda and Charles bundled them up and carted them home.

Moments later, the doctor returned. This time the news wasn't good.

"I'm afraid there isn't much, if any, circulation in her hands and feet," he told Wally, "We won't amputate yet because she needs to heal for awhile. In the meantime, we'll keep checking for a pulse, but I think that's what is ahead—amputations."

Wally's head spun. His knees buckled.

"I need to sit down," he said and slumped into a chair, stunned. Amputate? He had not seen this coming. "I thought she was past the crisis, that she was out of the woods."

"Do you remember what I told you about the Levophed?" the doctor asked. "It directs most of the blood supply to the vital organs and away from other body parts. That can cause the extremities to die from lack of blood flow. I think that's what we're seeing here."

For several days they monitored Loretta and adjusted her treatment. They gave her immunoglobulin to boost her immune system and started her on dialysis to flush the toxins and excess fluids from her body. Her cheekbones reappeared, and she started to look more like herself, although she was still unconscious. She had multiple ultrasounds of her limbs, looking for signs of circulation, and her family waited and waited and prayed. To begin her transition from IV nutrition to food, the doctor inserted a feeding tube that went directly into her stomach. Occasionally, Loretta's temperature would rise as she continued to fight the infection. She was still receiving Levophed, but was slowly being weaned from it.

Every day, the nurse changed the bandages on her hands and feet and pressed a stethoscope to her skin, listening for a pulse. One morning, she thought Loretta's right hand felt warmer, and she detected a pulse in her right wrist.

"And there's a fainter pulse in the left one, but it's not as strong as the right," she told Wally.

Loretta hovered in that suspended state, somewhere between here and not here. Whenever Mitch spoke to her or touched her arm, her eyes fluttered and struggled to open. Always, his voice triggered the same reaction. Sometimes she seemed to respond when the doctor asked her to move an arm or leg, and she even opened her eyes just a bit, though they didn't focus on anything or anyone. She coughed. Occasionally she kicked her legs or reached up to touch her face, and once, when Wally leaned down to kiss her on the forehead, she sprung up and bonked him on the chin.

"I love you Loretta," Wally said. If she was waking up, he wanted to be sure she heard his voice.

But Loretta slept on.

"We're all just sitting around waiting for her to wake up, and I have no idea how long it will be," Wally told her parents. "The kids need to get away from this hospital and have a real Christmas. Why don't you take them back to your house? Maybe it will get their minds off things for a while."

Back home in Shipman, Wanda and Charles devoted themselves to their grandchildren. Wanda made all the foods they loved to eat—mashed potatoes, green beans, pumpkin pie—and they helped her bake chocolate chip cookies. When they weren't busy in the kitchen, they tried to entertain the kids in other ways.

"Do you want to play a game with me and Grandpa?" Wanda asked.

"Okay, I guess," Alyssa replied and dug out the only game they hadn't played yet.

"They're trying to cheer us up," she whispered to Mitch.

"I know," he whispered back, "but I can't stop thinking about Mom."

For the first time, the Goebel family was separated on Christmas Eve, children from parents, husband from wife. Mitch and Alyssa attended church services with their grandparents and other family members. The church was filled with candles, holly, poinsettias, and sacred music, but all those trappings couldn't ease the mind of a worried child. When the congregation clasped hands to greet one another, Mitch turned around and shook his cousin's hand.

"Pray for my mom," he said softly. "I think she's going to die."

Chapter 8

Wally spent Christmas Eve at the control center. "I needed to get away from the hospital for a while," he told his co-worker. "You can't think about anything else—not doctors, not medicine, not infections—not when you're working with airplanes." For the next several hours he escaped his problems and was fully absorbed in his work, tracking aircraft and communicating with pilots.

The next morning he was back at Loretta's side. It didn't feel anything like Christmas. He missed the kids and their family traditions, missed the presents, missed the hot egg casserole Loretta always prepared—he missed it all.

"Merry Christmas!" the nurse announced, bright and chipper. She hustled over to take Loretta's temperature and blood pressure. "Are you okay?" she asked Wally.

"Merry Christmas," he replied, somber. "This isn't where I expected to be today."

"I know," the nurse answered. "But she seems to be doing better. Her vitals are right where they should be. Don't worry. This won't last forever." Wally already knew that it wouldn't last forever; he just didn't know what came next.

By early afternoon, Lisa and some other friends from church showed up with a CD player, a Bible, and some holy water, and they formed a circle around Loretta's bed to sing and pray. They hoped for a Christmas miracle, but still, Loretta slept. That is, until Lisa played one of Loretta's favorite hymns, "Shout to the Lord." Lisa cranked it up, and they all sang and cried, surrounding their friend with their love and prayers.

Almost immediately, tears flowed down Loretta's cheeks.

"Look," Lisa said. "She's crying! She can hear the music!"

"Loretta?" Wally called, leaning over her. "Can you hear me? Are you awake?"

Loretta briefly opened, then closed her eyes again. At that, the room erupted. Her friends embraced one another and jumped up and down, ecstatic. Until now, they didn't know if Loretta had suffered any brain damage, but she was crying, and this emotional response gave them hope that her brain was still functioning.

"She can hear us!" Wally said. "She knows what's going on!"

"I knew it!" Lisa added. "This song always makes her cry."

Wally grabbed the phone and dialed his in-laws' house. Wanda picked up and he shouted, "Loretta cried when we played Christmas music. She opened her eyes, and she could hear us! This is the best Christmas present I've ever had!"

Wanda put the receiver between Mitch and Alyssa, so they could both hear their dad. "Mom opened her eyes and cried. She's going to be okay," he told them, choking back his own tears.

"Can I talk to her?" Alyssa asked.

"Yeah, put her on the phone. Please Dad!" Mitch said.

"She's still not fully awake yet," Wally said. "But she's going to get well. You can stop worrying. Mom's going to get well."

Wha ... what is this?
Wally?

Loretta opened her eyes off and on, drifted in and out like the tide, but couldn't quite break through to full consciousness.

"Loretta? Can you hear me?" Wally called. He sounded so far away. She was at the bottom of a crater and he stood at the rim, calling down to her.

"Loretta?

Loretta?"

———

Who are all these ... where?
Hospital.

What happened?

———

"Her eyes are open again!" Lisa cried. "We love you, Loretta."

Every time Loretta fluttered her eyes, the room rejoiced. She was fighting to surface, and her friends cheered her on, laughing and hugging each other, smiling and clapping.

"Can you hear me, Loretta?" Wally asked, although he knew she couldn't answer. The ventilator was taped around her mouth, and it plunged down her throat.

She tilted her head toward his voice and grunted.

"Uuuugug..."

The room went wild. Until now, they thought the outcome would be one of two things: Loretta would either be dead, or she would be brain-dead.

She clearly wasn't either.

———

Wally ... Lisa
My mouth ....

It hurts ... get it out!
    Please ... help me

They're laughing.
Water!
        Help!

I need help ... they're laughing at me.

    Hospital.
            The ambulance, the tests, thumbs up.
            How long have I been asleep?

Get this thing OUT OF ME!

What happened?

    STOP LAUGHING AT ME!

Loretta floated in and out for the next couple of days, and each time she surfaced, Wally could see that she was disturbed. He tried to ease her mind. "You're in the hospital," he told her. "You've been very sick, but you're going to be okay now." He told her that she had been asleep for more than a week.

Gradually, Loretta came around and seemed a bit more alert each time she woke. Wally repeated what he'd told her earlier, but consumed by a drug-induced fog, she didn't understand. Her right arm and her side burned with intolerable pain, and she tried to tell Wally by signaling with grunts and grimaces. When he finally realized what she was trying to say, he alerted the nurse.

"Maybe the morphine isn't working," she said. "I'll call the doctor and see if we can switch her pain meds." She came back with a syringe of Dilaudid, a morphine derivative, which promptly gave Loretta the relief she needed.

But there was nothing they could do about her primary frustration. Loretta was clearly suffering on the ventilator, and over the next couple of days, she used hand gestures to communicate her misery. Her mouth was full of the tubing, and it was as dry as dust. Her throat was raw, irritated by the plastic tubes that pushed air in and out of her lungs.

"We can't take it out quite yet," the doctor told her. "We have to take baby steps to wean you off it little by little until you can breathe on your own. For now, we'll turn it down for short periods and monitor your oxygen levels. We'll take it out when it's safe."

Three days after Christmas, Loretta heard the magic words.

"Let's get you off that ventilator now," the doctor said, and they removed the tube from her throat. Loretta's eyes lit up, but she still couldn't do much more than grunt. When she realized they weren't going to put it back on, she tried out her voice. "I feel free," she told the nurse in a hoarse whisper.

Now that she was breathing on her own, Loretta felt hungry, but they had to introduce solid food in baby steps, too. Her first meal was a bowl of Jell-O—not exactly a feast, but it was a start. The nurse propped her up with pillows and fed her, and the cool, slippery concoction soothed her raw throat. Prior to this, she'd been lying down in bed, but now that she was sitting up, she saw her hands for the first time. They were completely covered with bandages. She didn't remember hurting them, but that didn't mean anything. There was a lot that she couldn't remember.

And what's going on with my legs? she wondered. She felt the compression pumps squeeze, then release, squeeze, then release her lower limbs. Loretta could talk a little now, but she wasn't ready to ask any questions. Not yet.

Waking up brought other rewards. After Mary had rushed to her bedside, she went back home and called Victoria's Secret. She knew that when Loretta woke up, she would want something pretty and feminine to wear, that she would need something to brighten her spirits. And she was convinced that Loretta would wake up.

"When Loretta gave Wally the thumbs up, I knew she'd come through," she told her husband, "because when Loretta says she'll do something, she does it." Mary ordered a pretty robe for her and had it delivered directly to the ICU, with instructions to give her the package as soon as she was conscious.

"This is the first time UPS has ever delivered a package from Victoria's

Secret to the ICU!" one of the nurses joked, as she pulled the gift from the closet. She gave the box to Loretta, but her hands were completely bandaged, and she couldn't open it.

"Laura, can you get this for me?" she asked her sister. Laura cut the paper and opened the box. She pulled out the delicate blue robe, and Loretta was moved to tears. "Leave it to Mary to think of something like this," she said. "She knew I'd want something pretty." Laura draped the robe around Loretta's shoulders, careful not to pull the sleeves over her bandaged hands.

Loretta had come a long way, but she still had a long way to go. Her family and friends went back to work and their regular responsibilities, but they juggled their schedules as best they could to relieve Wally at the hospital. Mitch and Alyssa were still with their grandparents, but Loretta's nephew, Brian, came to spend some time with her.

Brian lived in Nebraska. His grandfather on his dad's side had been critically ill, and he drove all the way from Lincoln to southern Illinois to be with him when he died. Afterward, Brian drove six hours north to see Loretta. Then he turned around and drove back to southern Illinois for his grandfather's funeral. He was only with her for a short time, but while he was there, he was very comforting.

"Your hair's kind of snarled," Brian said. "Can I brush it for you?"

"I don't know," Loretta said. "It's a complete mess from all the medicine they're giving me, and it's probably matted from lying in bed for so long. I don't know what you can do with it."

He picked up her hairbrush, sat on the side of the bed, and gently worked out some of the tangles. He ran the brush from her scalp to the ends nearly a thousand times, and Loretta relaxed in his tender attention.

"My mouth is so dry," she told him. "I'm still dehydrated. Can I have some ice chips?"

"I can't give you ice," he answered. "I'm supposed to swab your mouth with these little sponges. They're afraid the ice might make you sick."

"The sponges don't help. I really need ice. Please, just a little. I'll be fine."

So Brian fed her ice chips while they watched TV, violating the rules and catering to his aunt. After awhile, he asked a question.

"Why are your hands bandaged?"

"I don't know," Loretta answered. "I don't know anything about my hands."

The nurse came in, and Loretta asked her to take off the bandages. Slowly, she unspooled the gauze from her right hand. Something was seriously wrong; they all saw it. Her hand was black, like charcoal. Her cuticles were also black, but her fingernails were turning green, the color of the wicked witch from *The Wizard of Oz.* Her left hand looked exactly the same.

No one said a word. They stared at her hands, not breathing, not blinking, horror hanging over them.

Loretta broke the ice.

"This would make a good Halloween costume, wouldn't it?" she said. Then she raised her hands in the air, scrunched up her face, and said with a dramatic cackle, "I'll get you, my pretty!"

I am finally free of the ventilator and my nephew, Brian, stays with me all night. This is the first time I saw my hands. They are black! with curled fingers and black nails. My comment to Brian was that this would make a good Halloween costume ... not realizing that this was to be another part of my nightmare. I guess I thought it would heal, but ultimately only partial healing would occur and I would be scarred both physically and emotionally for the rest of my life.

Brian brushed my thinning hair, fed me ice chips and talked quietly with me all night.

Chapter 9

Loretta couldn't possibly understand the challenges that were ahead of her. She didn't even know the nature of her illness, and since she couldn't bring herself to ask any questions, she tried to figure it out for herself.

Whenever the nurses changed her bandages, she raised her bare hands to eye level and turned them from side to side, examining them as if they were foreign objects. Their long, slender shape was familiar, but she didn't recognize them. They were jet black and weren't getting any better. She tried to bend her fingers, but as soon as she did, she was sorry. An electric shock exploded from their tips and sparked like lightning all the way up to her elbows.

She could only think of one reason why her hands had turned black. *I've been burned,* she reasoned with herself. *I must have been in a fire. Did I dangle over the fires of hell?*

No one ever said anything to her about her hands—not the doctors, not the nurses, not Wally. She knew they had to stay bandaged and that she couldn't get them wet, but that was all she knew, all she wanted to know.

But her hands weren't the only concern. A string of scabs ran along the underside of her arm, where the ominous red line had signaled the infection. Blood and fluids had pooled at the surface of her skin, erupted, and scabbed over, leaving a wound that looked like one long, deep scratch. The incisions to drain her abscesses were still open, and they continued to leak out the toxins and infection. Every day, the nurses changed the gauze dressings.

"Ouch! That really hurts," Loretta complained when the nurse pulled off the tape. Her eyes filled with tears as she fought the pain.

"I know, I'm so sorry," the nurse said. "I'm trying not to hurt you."

When the dressings were off, Loretta looked down at her side and immediately wished she hadn't. She saw three large cavities, open and oozing.

"I'll never wear a bikini again," Loretta said with a catch in her voice. "I'm a mess."

"Oh, they'll stitch these up and they'll heal," the nurse soothed her. "You'll be surprised at how much they fade in a couple of months."

Eventually, Loretta went back to surgery to have the wounds closed. "Let's leave your bandages on for now," the nurse said, right before the orderlies wheeled her away. "They can take them off in the operating room when you're asleep." Loretta was grateful. She didn't want to endure that pain again.

The next day when she was back in her room, a thought struck Loretta. Her hands were black, and her side was a mess—what did the rest of her look like? She reached over and used her bandaged wrists to clamp hold of a hand mirror that was on her hospital tray. It was an awkward grab. She felt like she was wearing stiff boxing gloves, but she somehow managed to wedge the handle between her bulky hands.

She held the mirror up and took a good look. The swelling had subsided, and her face was thin and drawn. A large blood vessel had burst in her eye, and it blazed bright red, and there were two red marks that looked like cuts on either side of her mouth. She'd never seen those before.

"How did I get these marks?" she asked when a nurse stopped in to check her IV.

"That's where we secured the ventilator around your mouth," she said. "They'll fade, and your eye will return to normal, too. Just give it time."

When visitors came, Loretta put forth a positive front, but when she was alone, she lay awake and sobbed, particularly when she thought about her hands. Still confined to bed, the compression pumps continued to squeeze her legs to stimulate the circulation. *What's going on down there?* she wondered. She whipped off the blankets and discovered another nasty surprise. *My legs are bandaged!* she realized, alarmed. *Do they look like my hands?*

As the days progressed, her legs and hands started to burn from the inside out, and the pain was getting worse. It was excruciating—like fireworks exploding under her skin. Although the pain was actually a sign that her nerve endings were struggling to survive, Loretta was suffering and didn't know how much more she could endure. Soon her nights became unbearable.

The days weren't much better, either. They were, in fact, interminable. Wally had gone back to work, and Mitch and Alyssa were still at her parents' house. Loretta was bored, she was lonely, and she wanted to be in her own bed.

"I want to go home," she told anyone who would listen.

"Of course you do," the doctor said, "but we still need to keep an eye on you for a while longer."

The hospital staff was well aware of Loretta's distress, and Stephanie, her primary nurse, went to great lengths to relieve whatever suffering she could. She spent hours massaging Loretta's blackened limbs with lotion and, during those massages, she filled the room with relaxing Italian music.

"You'll probably be speaking Italian by the time you get out of here," she joked.

Stephanie combed through Loretta's hair, trying to remove the tangles that had once again built nests. One knot was so tight that even olive oil couldn't separate the strands, so with Loretta's permission, she snipped it out.

Loretta's unusual situation and her gentle personality had endeared her to her caregivers, and the rest of the staff went out of their way to take the edge off her hospital life, although she never asked for special treatment. She was low on calcium and needed to build up her reserves, so they gave her Tums to take as a supplement. But the hospital only carried peppermint, a flavor that made her nauseous. When her doctor heard that peppermint didn't agree with her, he made a special trip to the store and bought her some fruit-flavored Tums. One nurse brought in Loretta's favorite Bath and Body Works lotion because she noticed that she didn't like the medicinal smell of the hospital brand. And instead of the ugly, open-back hospital gowns, she was allowed to wear her own comfortable pajamas, and the nurses took the time to thread all the tubes up through her pajama legs and arms.

Lisa also brought Loretta a gift—a journal. She hoped it would help her pass the time, and she also thought it could be a way for Loretta to express her feelings. But how was she supposed to manage that? Her hands were wrapped and useless. At first Loretta didn't even try to write, but Wally helped her figure it out. He wedged a pen between her bandaged thumb and forefinger on her right hand, and she found that she could write if she moved her entire arm.

After some practice, her writing became legible.

During those empty days, Loretta had all the time in the world to obsess about Mitch and Alyssa. She thought about them. She worried about them. She dreamed about them. Beside herself with anguish, she pictured Wally telling them, "Mom may not make it," and it tore her apart. She knew she needed to direct her energy toward healing but, alone for hours, the sorrow consumed her.

It was a welcome break when Mary and her husband drove in from Cincinnati to visit. Now that she was improving, Mary wanted to see Loretta for herself. They settled in her room and chatted for a while, but Loretta was easily spent. She needed a nap. Even before she got sick, she had always indulged in a quick nap before the kids got home from school, and sleep was even more critical now. They left her to rest and went down to the cafeteria with Wally to get some coffee.

Loretta fell asleep in seconds, but awoke with a start, as if an internal alarm had chimed her awake. *The kids will be home any minute,* she thought, and she jumped off the bed. Her weak legs couldn't bear her weight, and they buckled beneath her. On her way down, her arms got tangled in the IV tubing and monitor cords and, like a marionette, she was suspended mid-air, too weak to call for help.

She hung there until a nurse walked by.

"Oh my gosh! What happened?" the nurse cried as she ran in to help. "Let me get you back in bed." She untangled the cords and eased Loretta back between the sheets. "Maybe we should restrain your arms so you don't fall out again," she suggested.

"No, no, I'm fine," Loretta said. "I was dreaming. I thought I was at home. I realize I'm in the hospital, and I need to stay in bed. I promise I won't do it again."

When she wasn't worrying about her children, Loretta agonized over her body. Sometimes she was afraid to fall asleep. She couldn't stop thinking about her hands and feet, and she prayed and prayed they would get better.

Meanwhile, Wally talked to her every day about her illness and often repeated the same information over and over, just to be sure she understood him. But he didn't want to burden her with more than she could handle, so he only told her what he thought was necessary.

"Just ask, and I'll tell you whatever you want to know," he said. "I will never lie to you." He explained that she'd had a bad infection and had almost died, but that she was much better now. It would take time, but she would get stronger.

"And no matter what, you will always have the best hands and feet we can get," he said. Loretta didn't know what he meant by that, but she didn't really want to know. She just nodded and didn't press for an explanation.

She talked to her doctor every day when he came in to review her chart and check on her progress. "I wish I could say that you'll make a complete recovery and walk out of this hospital," he said, "especially after the ordeal you've been through. But I still don't know what's ahead. We have to give it more time."

More time—that wasn't what she wanted to hear. With her in the hospital, Wally had far too much on his shoulders, and she worried about him. He had to keep the house in order, pay the bills, shop for groceries, go to work, update the family, plus he visited her every day after work—and then drove forty-five minutes back home. And she knew he was sick with worry about her. She was a burden to him now, she just knew it. *Try not to cry in front of him,* she admonished herself, but at the same time, she desperately needed his emotional support.

"Could you just hold me?" she asked him. She scooted over as far as possible to make room for him on the bed. Wally sat down and put his arms around her shoulders, careful not to pull on any of the wires. He rested his chin on the top of her head and held his wife. He needed this, too, needed to be close to her as much as she needed him. He felt nearly as helpless as she was.

"It'll be okay," he whispered. "We'll figure this out. You'll come home before long." But it was almost New Year's Eve, and Loretta knew she wasn't going home any time soon.

I am afraid to sleep at night. The nights in the hospital are so long and my black hands and feet scare me! I pray to Jesus to heal me, to take the black away! I pray for "pink feet"!!

Why are my hands and feet black? I don't understand what has happened to me! Is this a dream? Please wake me up!

I can't wait for Wally to come to see me! I need him near me! I am scared and upset about how I must look!

I am told I had surgery. I have 3 long open areas on my right side. Surgeries for what? What has happened?

my hands and feet are in pain. The
pain can't compare to the pain I
had in my heart when I think
about Mitch and Alyssa being told
that their mom may not come home.
I can't imagine how they felt
when they came to see me.
Hooked up to countless machines,
"blown up like a balloon"
(Alyssa's description) and non responsive.
We are a close family and the
"I love you's" are always said
And I couldn't say it. I had
told them I loved them before
they left for the Christmas program
but would it have lasted them
their life time if I hadn't come home?

Wally promised me that he would tell me the truth of all of this but do I want to know?

He's telling me I will always have the best hands and feet we can get. What is he saying?

The pains in my hands and feet are intense. I can press a button for medication to come through my IV. What is going on in my limbs? Are they slowly dying or are they trying to wake up? Oh, please be the latter!

Chapter 10

New Year's Eve had always been a special night for Loretta and Wally. When she worked at the Hyatt, she planned the annual New Year's Eve party, and when the evening finally arrived, Loretta was in her element. The ultimate hostess, she checked on the dinner, visited with guests, and made sure the band had everything they needed. She rarely stopped for more than a minute. Wally came along and pitched in to help wherever he was needed, usually functioning as the barback who ran to the kitchen to get more garnishes—olives, sliced lemons, and limes—so the bartender didn't have to leave his station. He also picked up empty plates and glasses, and ended up mingling with the guests and enjoying the live music. And, of course, Loretta stopped to chat and flirt with him throughout the night. After the kids were born, they spent New Year's Eve a little closer to home at a neighborhood party, or they went out to dinner and then cozied up by their own fire.

This year was understandably different, but Loretta still wanted to celebrate. She was gradually recovering; in fact, she was strong enough to move out of ICU. Her doctor put her in a room on the oncology ward, where the air was carefully filtered for germs and communicable diseases. Since her immune system was still dangerously weak, he gave her a private room that was equipped with special air filters to minimize her risk of contracting other infections.

Loretta wanted this New Year's Eve to be as festive as possible, but the best option they had was to pick out a movie from the hospital cart. "Let's get a musical, something fun and lively," she said. "Do they have *Grease?*" Wally climbed up next to her, and they got lost for a couple of hours in the familiar music and story they'd seen so many times before. When the movie was over, it was only ten-thirty, not yet the magical midnight hour, but Wally had a long drive home. Since he was working the next day, they agreed he shouldn't stick around for a midnight kiss.

Out of all her nights in the hospital, this was the one night that Loretta especially didn't want Wally to leave. She thought back to all their previous New Year's Eve celebrations and how she'd get all decked out in a fancy dress and heels, fix her hair and makeup, and spritz on special perfume. When they got home after the evening's festivities, they would make love, bringing in the New Year by making that ultimate connection. It was a lot to lose.

"I don't want you to leave," she said when he got up to get his coat.

"I wish I didn't have to." He bent down and kissed her twice, once for goodbye, and once for the New Year.

When Wally shut the door, an empty ache consumed her. Like a lurking predator, the grief pounced, landing smack in the middle of her heart. She cried over her husband, her lover, her equal. She missed her children and missed her life. The tears she had so carefully concealed descended like a hard rain, and she convulsed with sobs until, around midnight, she finally fell asleep.

Wally had to work on New Year's Day, but he didn't want to leave Loretta alone, so he arranged for a variety of friends to visit her at regular intervals. "Surprise!" the first group called as they came in her room, and just as they were leaving, the next group arrived. All day long, her friends and neighbors streamed in, bringing her simple, thoughtful gifts, like a pink feather boa and a box of Fruit Loops, Loretta's favorite cereal. No one came empty-handed.

"I'm sorry, but we'll have to take that out," the nurse said, pointing to an English ivy that had somehow gotten past the nurse's station. "She can't have any plants or flowers in her room right now," the nurse explained, "not until her immune system is stronger. You never know what allergens might be hiding in these leaves, and we don't want to compromise her recovery."

The visitors continued to file in. Loretta enjoyed it, and she knew that Wally meant well, but after awhile, she was drained. Like a hostess at a party, she felt she had to entertain her guests, until she finally reached the point of exhaustion. Ultimately, her friends realized how tired she was, and one-by-one, they extended their New Year's wishes and left. When the last person finally closed the door, she shut her eyes.

For the next several days she continued to improve and slipped into a routine of meals, visits from doctors and nurses, daily sponge baths, and time with Wally. Friends and neighbors stopped by in random fashion, which always boosted her spirits. In private, she continued to pray that her hands and feet would heal, although the longer she lay in bed, the less likely it seemed they would get better.

At last, Mitch and Alyssa came home. They were so excited to see their mother that Charles and Wanda could barely hold them back. They shot down the hall, but when they got to her room, they stopped in their tracks, suddenly shy. They weren't used to their mom being sick, and even though she was awake now, she was still in this big, sterile hospital, and they didn't like it. They sized her up from the doorway. She wasn't puffed up anymore, so she looked like their mom again, albeit a little tired. Then she flashed them her monster-sized smile and thrust out her arms, and the barrier was broken. They crossed the threshold, but as they got closer, they saw her wrapped hands and scarlet eye, and they hesitated again.

"What's wrong with your eye, Mommy?" Alyssa asked. Her cherub face was wrinkled with concern, and she seemed a little frightened.

"It's okay, honey," Loretta told her. "I know it's really red, but that will go away in a few days. It's already getting better." Loretta knew she would be dealing with a number of problems, but she doubted her eye would be one of them.

That explanation was enough, and the children broke free and ran to her bed. Loretta embraced them as best as she could. She laid her head on top of theirs, and was swept away by their clean smell and soft hair. It had been a lifetime since she had held her children.

After the initial hugs, the kids turned their attention to the stack of Christmas and get-well cards that had piled up on her nightstand.

"You sure have a lot of cards," Mitch said.

Alyssa grabbed a few of them and asked, "Can I read them to you?"

"That sounds great," Loretta said, and they all listened as Alyssa read card after heartfelt card. It took quite a while for her to get through even a small part of the stack, but they were content to be together, no matter what they were doing. Mitch reached over every now and then and patted his mom on the shoulder, filling her with a love so intense she thought her heart would burst.

Now that Wally had gone back to work, Loretta's parents and sisters arranged their schedules so that someone would be with Loretta as much as possible. Laura drove the four hours from her home as often as she could. They were still best friends, as well as sisters, and their conversation came easy.

"So where's my new puppy?" Loretta asked her.

"What new puppy?" Laura asked.

"You told me I was getting a new puppy for Christmas," Loretta said. "What kind is it?"

Laura thought back over everything she had said to Loretta while she was unconscious, and she knew she never said she was getting a puppy. Loretta didn't even like dogs; there was no way anyone would buy her a puppy.

"You aren't getting a puppy," she explained, "but Justin and Jessica did. That's what I told you—that we were getting our kids a puppy for Christmas. But, wow! That means you could hear me talking to you."

"I remember some things people were saying, but everything's all scrambled, like in a dream," Loretta said.

Later, as Laura got ready to leave, Loretta said, "By the way, when you come in tomorrow you should check out the incredible spa they have here."

"And what spa is that?" Laura asked, stifling a laugh.

"I'm not sure how you get to it, but I had my hair washed, and they put me in this wonderful pool of water," Loretta told her. "It was lovely. The water was really warm and there was music."

For a brief moment, Laura thought she should look around the hospital for this magnificent spa because Loretta was quite adamant about it. But she'd never heard of a hospital that had a spa.

"I don't think there's anything like that at the hospital," Laura said with some skepticism.

But Loretta insisted. "Yes, there is! While my hair was being washed, I could see Tim McGraw, and I could hear him singing. It was an island setting, and there were seahorses floating everywhere." Loretta paused to think about what she had just described. "Okay, maybe it wasn't exactly like that, but I know there's a nice spa around here somewhere."

Loretta couldn't let it go and later, she asked Wally about when she had her hair washed at the spa.

"Um … that's not actually what happened," he said. "The nurses just pulled you to the end of the bed and washed your hair over a garbage bag that caught all the soap and water."

She shook her head, confused. "It all seemed so glamorous," she said, still not convinced that she remembered it wrong.

Loretta's wild memories were probably a result of her medications and the infection, as was her continued, excessive thirst, which frustrated her on several levels. She wanted to be able to get a sip of water whenever she wanted and didn't want to wait for help. The longer she lay in bed waiting for someone else to help her, the more aggravated she got.

"Could you please get me some kind of gription tape for my hands?" she asked Stephanie, her nurse. "I want to put it over these bandages, so I can pick up my cup.

"Gription tape?" Stephanie repeated. "What's that?"

"I don't know," she answered, frustrated. "I need some kind of Velcro or something, so I can grab stuff. Something that will grip onto a cup—because I can't pick up anything with these clunky mitts on!"

"I've never heard of anything like that," Stephanie said, "but let's see what we can rig up." And they did. They put one strip of Velcro on her cup and another on her bandages, and after that, Loretta could get her own drink. It was a small step to becoming a bit more self-sufficient and, in her eyes, to be slightly less of a burden on others. She couldn't wait to show the kids when they came to celebrate Mitch's birthday.

Everyone has just one golden birthday—the birthday when their age matches their birth date—and Mitch was turning ten on January 10. Loretta was a meticulous planner and had been preparing for this special occasion for quite some time. She had already bought and wrapped his birthday presents long before Christmas and well before she got sick. But the bowling party she'd originally planned wasn't an option now. They'd have to celebrate in her hospital room.

Loretta always dressed up for family celebrations, and she was eager to do so now, thinking it would help her feel more like her old self. She knew it bothered Alyssa to see her with stringy hair and pasty skin, and then there was her eye, still bloodshot and blazing. Sometimes Loretta caught her daughter staring at her, as if she was trying to find her real mom somewhere inside the woman in the hospital bed. Perhaps if she dressed up for the party, Alyssa would see a glimmer of the mom she was missing.

Two of Loretta's friends helped her get ready. They put her in a reclining chair and rolled her into the shower area, washed and fixed her hair, and plucked her eyebrows. Wally brought in her makeup bag, and they used some recent pictures to copy how she applied her makeup. She felt fresh, and she knew she looked better than she had in weeks. It was starting to feel like a celebration.

Loretta's mom was back in town, and she had baked an angel food cake for Mitch's birthday. Before they lit the candles on the cake, Wally took the kids down to the cafeteria to get pizza—hospital pizza.

"This is so unfair to Mitch," Loretta told Wanda. "His golden birthday shouldn't be in a hospital room."

"He's just glad you're doing better," Wanda said. "You know kids. They go with the flow. He probably thinks it's an adventure just because it's different. Don't worry about it."

When they got back, Wally offered Loretta and Wanda a piece of pizza, and Mitch opened his gifts. Alyssa stood near Loretta and watched her brother tear open his presents. He seemed happy, and both kids appeared to be having fun, but Loretta wasn't convinced. *How can a hospital room and hospital pizza be any fun on your golden birthday?* she thought. Later, Alyssa told her it was pretty awful.

Loretta tried to savor every moment, but a dark cloud settled over her that wouldn't lift. She dreaded the moment when her family would leave again, when she would plunge back into the stark loneliness of her hospital life. *Stop thinking about it,* she scolded herself. *Just try to have fun while they're here.* Despite her best efforts, she couldn't muster up her normal party self.

Ten days later, the doctor approached Wally. "It's been more than three weeks, and her circulation has not improved," he said. "We need to consider amputation. I think it's the only option."

For whatever reason, Wally never really believed they would amputate. He kept thinking she would somehow fully recover. He rubbed his forehead, pushing back the pain.

"I don't know," he said. "I don't even know what's involved. I know it means you want to cut off her hands and legs, but what would actually happen?"

"The legs would be a transtibial, or below-the-knee amputations," the doctor said, "which is the most common type of limb removal and is often a result of diabetes. We'll make an incision and then divide the muscle, so that the leg bones—the tibia and fibula—can be cut with a special saw. Then the muscles and skin are wrapped back over the end of the cut bones and sewn shut."

Wally felt sick. Had it really come to this? There was no way he could tell Loretta. He had never mentioned the word "amputation" to her, and he knew he could never utter that word, not to the woman he loved—and he didn't have to. The next day before Wally even arrived, several doctors assembled in her room. The orthopedic surgeon took the lead.

"We've waited to see if the circulation would return to your hands and feet, but it hasn't," he began. "These items need to be amputated. I've scheduled you for surgery tomorrow, and now I'd like to talk to you about hand transplants."

Loretta recoiled. Her eyes glazed, and she was struck silent. Both the message and the messenger were repulsive. The doctor, a short man with inky dark hair, had a distinguishing feature she'd never seen outside a horror movie: He had a hunchback. She sensed his eerie, mad scientist demeanor and pictured him cutting off her hands and placing them in a jar in his basement for his own private collection. She felt like Igor himself was standing next to her bed, panting after her parts.

He was not only physically frightening, but his bedside manner was deplorable. Without an ounce of compassion or normal sensitivity, he abruptly spouted off about her "items," and hand amputations, and even more shocking—would she consider a hand transplant?

At this point, Loretta still didn't fully understand what had happened to her. She couldn't possibly make the jump from being sick to agreeing to amputations, to having her feet and hands whacked off in one fell swoop—a surgery that had already been scheduled for the following day. And she'd never even heard of a hand transplant!

She stared at him in horror. She thought she had mentally prepared herself for the worst, had told herself that she would probably have limited use of her hands, and even thought she might end up in a wheelchair, but she never, ever considered *AMPUTATIONS!*

She said nothing.

"Think about it," he urged her. "Talk it over with your husband."

Loretta didn't need to do any thinking, but she did do some talking when Wally arrived a few minutes later. Normally a gracious and benefit-of-the-doubt kind of person, she was adamant, and she was loud.

"That doctor will **NEVER** come in my room again!"

But that wasn't the end of it. The doctor had dispatched a counselor who came in to discuss her amputations and the possibility of hand transplants. The very idea abhorred her. It was frightening to think about walking around wearing someone else's hands, and they asked the woman to leave.

Wally felt miserable about these conversations and their impact on Loretta, and he owed her an explanation. "Seeing your tears on Christmas Day was the best gift I've ever received," he reminded her. "And I knew we were going to have a rough road ahead of us. They did mention that amputations might be necessary because of the Levophed, but you would have died without it. I told them it didn't matter, to give it to you anyway. I just wanted you to survive. It's going to be hard, Loretta, but you're here. You're alive, and I love you."

"But how will I be able to do anything?" she asked. "If I can't walk and I don't have any hands, how can I take care of the kids?" She pictured herself wearing a hook, and her whole body responded with an involuntary shudder.

"Like I told you before, you'll have the best hands and feet we can find," he said. "We'll make it work. But you will not have surgery tomorrow, and you won't see that doctor again. We'll get a second opinion before we do anything." He sat on the bed and cradled his wife in his arms. The mixture of comfort and sadness, of grief and paralyzing fear, overwhelmed them both, and clutching one another, they wept.

Behind the scenes, Wally and Mary had already been researching other surgeons, but Wally was a little reluctant to tell her doctors—the ones who had saved Loretta's life—that they wanted a second opinion. But they had no choice. Amputations were so final.

"I don't blame you," her lead doctor said. "If it was my wife, I'd do the same thing. I'll connect you with someone at the university hospital." He soon returned to Loretta's room with an appointment for her to see a top vascular surgeon.

Even though she still had the catheter inserted and was pitifully frail, Wally wheeled her out of the hospital and lifted her into his truck. When they arrived at the new hospital, Loretta waited in the wheelchair, her two-inch-thick chart on her lap. The new doctor looked over the first few pages, then asked, "How would you like to stay with us for a few days?"

Wally pushed her to the waiting room where they were supposed to stay until her room was assigned. Six hours later, her doctor walked by, appalled to see that they were still sitting there. Loretta was slumped over in the wheelchair, and Wally's head leaned on the back of the sofa. The doctor called for an orderly.

"Take these folks up to our VIP floor," he said. "They've been here way too long, and Mrs. Goebel needs to lie down."

He escorted them to a floor with private rooms that were furnished in cherry wood, usually reserved for their high-end clients. "Wow," Loretta said. Even in her diminished state, she noticed the elaborate furnishings and how unhospital-like it was. It felt more like the Hyatt than a hospital.

"Let me help you," one nurse said to her.

"Can I get you anything?" asked another.

Most of the other patients on that floor had brought their own private nurses, so several staff nurses were available for Loretta. They made sure she was as comfortable as possible, and she felt like a guest rather than a patient.

This was a teaching hospital, and the next morning during rounds, the orthopedic surgeon brought a group of second- and third-year medical students to her room. The students seemed reluctant to touch her. None of them had ever seen a case like hers, but neither had most of the physicians. The surgeon showed the students how to bandage Loretta's feet and hands—tight enough to protect them, but loose enough so they could breathe.

"I feel like I'm in show-and-tell," she told Wally, but she didn't really mind the extra scrutiny.

Three days later, the vascular surgeon completed his analysis and gave them the results. "There's no rush to amputate. There's no gangrene and no infection. The black areas are simply dead tissue," he said. "I'm going to send you home to give your body a chance to heal. Some of your circulation may still return, at least to a portion of your limbs.

"I think it's worth the wait, don't you?"

How many 10 year olds have had to
celebrate their "golden birthday" in
a hospital room with their mom in
a bed with bandaged hands and feet &
IV's? He never complained... never
asked about his usual bowling party
with friends. I know that we were
happy to be together that night but
my heart hurt for Mitch and how
it could and should have been.

❦

Dr. Bone is saddened by my state
of affairs. He wishes he could say
I'll be alright and can walk
out of the hospital on my own,
especially after what I have
already been through. But that
is not the case and what is
instore is still uncertain.

my heart hurts! Am I going
to lose my hands and feet?
I am a busy mom. A stay-at-home
mom who is never home! I need
my hands and feet! PLEASE, Lord, please!!

PART TWO

On the Chopping Block

Life is not easy for any of us.
We must have perseverance and above all, have confidence in ourselves.
We must believe that we are gifted for something, and that this thing, at whatever cost, must be attained.

~ Madame Marie Curie

Chapter 11

After more than a month in the hospital, Loretta was finally going home. The nurse helped her get dressed, and together they packed up everything that had accumulated in her room. Hundreds of cards and get-well wishes, photographs, and drawings sent from schoolchildren were put in a box, and they stuffed her pajamas, toiletries, and other belongings in a plastic bag. Finally, the doctor gave her the okay. The papers were signed, and they were on their way home.

Of all the things that Loretta had missed while she was in the hospital, missing Christmas was one of the worst. All of her meticulous planning and extravagant preparations had been for nothing; the holidays had come and gone. With presents still wrapped and under the tree, they decided they would celebrate Christmas that night, her first night home. Her parents were in town taking care of the kids, and when her friends and neighbors heard she would arrive around dinner time, they prepared for her homecoming, too.

It was a dark drive on the highway, but when they turned into their neighborhood, Loretta gasped. Their street was all lit up, and it sparkled like a winter wonderland. Their neighbors had left their decorations and Christmas lights up, anticipating the day when Loretta would finally come home. One house was topped with Santa and his reindeer. The next displayed colorful carolers. To the right, Loretta saw a life-sized manger scene complete with Mary, Joseph, and baby Jesus, along with the three kings and all the traditional animals. Hickory Circle was a cornucopia of snowmen, Christmas trees, decorations, and lights. It was magical.

"Oh Wally," she cried out. "It's beautiful."

"Merry Christmas," Wally said softly.

"I can't believe they kept Christmas alive this long, just for me," she said in awe.

Their own house was ahead. Months ago she had hung a fresh holly and pinecone wreath on the front door and had dressed all the front-facing windows with wreaths suspended from red velvet ribbons. The wreath on the dining room window had been hard to install; it measured six feet in diameter. Crisp white lights framed their house, and they sparkled like sequins in the frosty Illinois night.

They pulled in the garage, and Wally carried her inside and sat her at the kitchen table, where Loretta's parents were waiting. Mitch and Alyssa jumped up and ran to her.

"Mommy!" Alyssa cried.

"Hi, Mom," Mitch said, a little more reserved.

She wrapped her arms around them both and inhaled deeply, breathing in their familiar child scents, and she sobbed and sobbed, so happy to be home, so grateful to be back in her own kitchen. Her tears dripped from her face onto theirs. Wanda and Charles shed their own tears, and Wally's eyes puddled. She was finally home—wounded, yet intact; different, but the same; alive, but almost lost.

She gazed around her kitchen. The Christmas tree stood in the corner, right where she left it. Its soft glow warmed the room. Dinner was on the stove, and the smell of chicken baking coupled with the sound of her children laughing was so satisfying that it pained Loretta deep inside her chest, down to the recesses of her heart. The warmth and color of her home was such a welcome sight after the stark, white cold of the hospital. She was home.

Wanda had fixed mashed potatoes and corn to go with the chicken—comfort food they all craved. They sat at the table, but since Loretta couldn't use her hands, her mother fed her, relishing the old, familiar act. She lifted the spoon to her daughter's mouth and was reminded of when she was a baby, how she was always happy and almost always cooperative. Loretta's pleasant personality emerged early, and it never changed. She had always been lovely.

"It's so good to be home," Loretta said between bites.

"We're glad you're here, too, Mommy," said Alyssa. "I don't ever want you to leave again."

They finished eating, and Mitch and Alyssa couldn't wait to open their presents. Wally helped Loretta get in the wheelchair and pushed her into the family room, silently thankful that their doorways and halls were wide enough to accommodate it. The gifts were piled under the tree in the family room, most of them wrapped by Loretta herself when she still had hands that could wrap. Her mind spun as if in a time warp. The memory of Christmas preparations clashed with her hospital life. Had she really done all this? She could hardly remember.

The children laughed and chattered while they filled their mom in on the details of their friends and activities at school. Alyssa passed out the gifts, and they each took a turn to open all their presents and take center stage, just like they'd done every other year. The kids helped Loretta unwrap hers, and just as Alyssa's turn ended, the doorbell rang.

Wally wheeled Loretta into the foyer and opened the door. About twenty people stood outside, bundled up in heavy coats, scarves, and mittens. They spilled off the porch and onto the lawn, each face illuminated by the soft sheen of a candle. They were her neighbors and friends from church, and Lisa was at the head of the pack.

"Merry Christmas," they called out in unison. "Welcome home!"

Loretta looked at the crowd. These were her friends, her true friends—the ones who were there in times of trouble, the ones she could truly count on. They serenaded her with "Silent Night," and overhead, the stars twinkled in the cold, clear sky. Fresh snow hushed the night, and their sweet, clear voices rang out like a choir of angels. Neighborhood fireplaces burned. The oaky, smoky smell filled Loretta's nostrils and completed the perfect Christmas scene. Tears streamed down her face.

Wally leaned down behind her, put his head on hers, and encircled her in his arms. She felt a tear fall from his face, and he wiped them from both her eyes and his. Mitch and Alyssa stood quiet, their eyes also glistening. Wanda and Charles stood behind them, and were touched to see that even though the Goebels didn't have any "real" family in Sycamore, they had, in fact, created an extended one that loved them without reserve.

Twenty minutes and several songs later, the carolers waved goodbye. "We love you Loretta," they called out. Lisa bent down to kiss her cheek.

"Thank you so much," Loretta said. "I love you, Lisa. You don't know how much this meant to me."

After they left, Loretta was emotionally drained and physically exhausted. Wally carried her upstairs and sat her in the playroom recliner, the exact same spot where she had nursed her aching arm before they went to the emergency room. He went back downstairs, lugged up the wheelchair, then pushed her down the hall to the master bathroom, where he and Wanda helped her bathe. Wally dried her off, then brushed her teeth.

Loretta couldn't wait to get in her own bed. In the hospital, she had fantasized about this moment so many times, had waited for this pleasure for what seemed like an eternity. Wally laid her down under her own covers, her head resting on her own pillow. Her mattress was so soft, and the cream and burgundy flannel sheets were warm and cozy. She was certain her mom had just washed them because they smelled so clean and fresh, so perfect. Overwhelmed by the comfort, she dissolved into tears.

The lights sparkled on the trees in their bedroom and sitting room. Wally climbed in beside her and wrapped her in his arms. He kissed her tears, kissed her neck, and very gently, with a full heart, he made love to his wife. He was tender, extremely cautious, as if they had never made love before. Tears rolled down his cheeks and mingled with hers. At that moment, Loretta didn't think about her hands and feet, black and bandaged, not when she was with Wally. She was completely overcome with home and husband, snuggling and sleep.

But the next day they woke up, and in the harsh glare of the morning, they were smacked back to reality. Wally had to rush off to work, but before he left, he asked, "Do you need to go potty first?" He brought her the bedpan and set it on the sheets.

The spell was broken. The woman she had been the night before—sexy and loved, cradled in her husband's arms—didn't exist in the morning. This was the truth: Loretta was the patient, and Wally was the caregiver.

Chapter 12

Because Loretta needed ongoing attention and the kids needed someone to take care of them, both sets of grandparents took turns helping out in a shuffle they called "The Changing of the Grandmas." Wally's parents drove six hours from Michigan, and when they went back home, Loretta's parents drove the four hours from Shipman, an exchange that took place every two weeks.

Mitch and Alyssa went back to school early in January. It was a welcome change, but they felt barraged by questions from their teachers, other parents, and even their schoolmates.

"Every day people ask so many questions about you," Alyssa told her mother. "I don't like it. I don't know what to say."

Loretta knew they asked questions out of concern, but she had hoped that school would be the one place where life would seem normal, especially since their home life had been turned upside down. She wished people wouldn't discuss her situation and prognosis with her children. She talked to Wally, and they came up with a standard response the kids could offer. "Just tell them she's doing better and she's at home now," Wally said. "You don't have to say more than that."

Answering questions about her mom wasn't the only thing that upset Alyssa. Loretta had always been involved in her school activities, but now there were some events that she simply couldn't attend. The annual sock hop was coming up and was something the whole school looked forward to, but there was no way that Loretta could go this year. She encouraged Alyssa to go with a friend and her mother, which she did. When she got home, Loretta asked her to demonstrate all the steps she had learned. "Now I know what to practice for next year," Loretta told her, though deep down she didn't think she would ever dance again.

One day, Alyssa asked her mother a direct question. "Mom, why can't you walk anymore?"

Loretta tried to find words a seven-year-old would understand. "While I was sick, my feet died," Loretta said. "But it's going to be okay because I didn't die, and that's the most important thing."

"Can you feel your feet?" Alyssa asked.

"I don't really have much feeling in them. I can't move them, but they do hurt a little," Loretta said. "And one day I will walk again. Maybe not on the legs God gave me, but on new ones that a doctor makes for me."

In the end, Loretta's explanation seemed to satisfy Alyssa's curiosity for the moment, but she still didn't truly understand what had happened to her mother.

Loretta was still very weak. Her vitamin storage had been completely depleted, and she needed to regain her strength. In the mornings, she woke up totally spent, so she kept protein bars and Ensure shakes beside her bed that she ate and drank when she first woke up. She literally needed that extra energy to get going. Every night, Wally had to inject blood thinners directly into her abdomen, in order to increase the blood flow and decrease the risk of clots. The first time, his hand shook so much he could barely complete the task.

Things seemed to be going fairly well, but under the surface, something was brewing. Loretta couldn't stand it that she had to depend on others for everything. In fact, it was suffocating. She had been completely self-sufficient before and was always the first one to get up in the mornings. She loved that time alone before the day became chaotic and would sit and have a cup of coffee, using that quiet time to meditate and pray.

Now she couldn't even get out of bed by herself. She had to wait for the grandmother-in-residence to help her and, even then, it wasn't easy. In order to get into the wheelchair, she had to scoot over to a transfer board that they leaned against the side of the bed. She then slid down the board and into the wheelchair, but she couldn't do it unless someone guided her.

After about three weeks of this, she got tired of waiting. Wally's parents weren't back from seeing the kids off on the bus, and she wanted to get out of bed. She wanted to get up and do something—anything! She remembered how her baby niece got out of bed by sliding off on her tummy and decided to try it herself.

She rolled over on her stomach and slid off the side of bed and onto her knees. Dragging her black, useless legs behind her, she made her way down the hall to the playroom and climbed into the recliner. A little later, Wally's mother, Penny, came upstairs, and Loretta watched her go down the hall to the master bedroom. Loretta didn't say a word. Penny popped back out, and ran down the hall, frantically calling Loretta's name, looking first in the bathroom, then in every other room that lined the hall. She laughed when she found Loretta in the recliner and was obviously relieved.

"I didn't know where you were!" she said.

"I'm right here," Loretta said with a smile, proud of her accomplishment.

Penny knew that with Loretta's determined spirit, nothing could keep her down, and that day proved to be a turning point. After that, Loretta went everywhere on her knees.

Proud of her innovation, Loretta called to brag to Laura, who tried walking on her own knees to see how it felt. Laura thought about the situation. Loretta's house was carpeted upstairs, but it might hurt to get around on the tile and hardwood floors on the main level, so she went to Target and looked for the kneepads she'd seen in the gardening section. She pulled them off the shelf and tried them on, then got down on her knees and walked up and down the aisle. The other shoppers stared at her. Some were curious; others just looked amused, but Laura didn't care what they thought. She just wanted Loretta to be comfortable. Satisfied they would work, she bought the kneepads, packed them up, and sent them overnight via Federal Express.

Loretta was delighted. Her mother-in-law strapped them on her, and they were perfect. The hard floors didn't bruise her kneecaps anymore.

Normally during The Changing-of-the-Grandmas, there was a two-hour window on Saturday when Wally was at work and Loretta was at home alone with the kids. This was her time to be on her own, to feel like Mom again, and to tend to her own house. She didn't want to tell the grandmas that she liked her bath towels folded a different way than they had folded them, so she reached her bandaged hands high, straining to reach the towel shelf from her knees, and pulled them all down on the bathroom floor. It was a struggle, but she got them all refolded. There was no way she could put them back by herself, and she had to get the kids to help her, but she felt like she'd reclaimed a small piece of her territory. Loretta didn't want to seem unappreciative, but it was the hundreds of little things—like the towels—that made her feel out of control of her life and her home.

On one of those Saturdays, Mitch and Alyssa wanted to go out to play in the snow. Mitch called up the stairs, "Are you okay if we both go outside?"

"Sure, I'm fine," she called back. "Go right ahead."

She walked to the window on her knees to watch them, her chin barely clearing the sill. She started to cry. Something was very wrong with this situation. She should be the one worried about them and checking on them, instead of the other way around. She longed to do what she had always done, to go outside and watch them play, to throw some snowballs and make a snowman, then fix hot chocolate when they came inside, but it looked like those days were over.

❦

Dr. Pierce says I can go home and get my strength up. It is being said that my legs will be amputated below the knees. What!?!
Dr. Rana is ready to schedule.
I just want to go home!
I am afraid to go though of how my conditions might upset the kids.
Wally says it will be OK.
We arrive home! My eyes fill with tears! Wally carries me into the kitchen. It is dinner time and the kids and mom and Dad are happy to see us. We all eat together. Thank you, God!
The kids watch as I hold my

Silverwear with my new 'tubes' –
Lindsay, from Rockford, set me
up with different size tubes to
hold ink pens, silverwear etc.

Sleep in my own bed! I am
so excited to lay in my own
bed next to my husband! I
won't be able to sleep!

~~xxxxxxxxxx~~

I am picked up into bed and
slide out on a slant board
into the wheelchair. "
I cannot express how heavy
my heart is. I am so happy to

be home, but this is not how I want
to live!

I wake in the mornings and am
so weak! my htamh storage in
my body was drained in this
illness and I am trying to build it
back up with prokin bars and
boost.
my stomach has shrank so I
can only eat small amounts at
once. Therefore, I requested
to eat 4-5small meals instead
of trying to eat enough at 3.

I am not sleeping well as the pain
wakes me up. I have to take

medicine but when the pain that shoots
into your foot makes your leg
jerk, you need something to
take the edge off to sleep.
I can usually tolerate the
pain in the day, but come
evening I am at wits end.
Tears behind the eye balls could
come flooding down if I
would allow, but I am
trying to be strong for the kids.

I wake up early and it all
seems so normal and then
I remember the reality and
feel sick.
"Come on, get up, the kids need you!"

Chapter 13

When Linda, Loretta's older sister, came back to visit, she could see that Loretta was suffering, and that she was at her wits' end from being totally dependent on everyone else. It would have been bad enough if only her legs were affected, but Loretta couldn't use her hands, which multiplied her misery. She had lost every shred of privacy. She needed help to use the toilet, to take a bath, to get dressed, to brush her teeth, and fix her hair. She couldn't eat without assistance, nor could she make a phone call or even blow her nose. Even the tiniest of tasks were beyond her, and on top of all that, Loretta was in deep pain.

It was hard to watch. Linda remembered all the prayers she had said when Loretta was sick, begging God to spare her. Now she wondered if those prayers had condemned her sister to the life of an unhappy invalid.

They were sitting together one afternoon, and before she even spoke, Linda started to cry. "I need to ask you something." She looked at Loretta. "Was it wrong of me to pray for you to live? I look at what you have to deal with now, and I can't help but wonder if you wish we hadn't prayed for you."

Loretta was shocked. "No!" she said. "Absolutely not!" She took a breath and continued, "Linda, if I had died at that point, it would have been okay because, despite my many flaws, I truly feel like I had a clean heart. I loved my life. I wasn't holding anything back from anyone, I wasn't harboring hate, I wasn't envious or jealous—I just loved my life.

"But God took care of me, and it wasn't my time. I need to be here for Mitch and Alyssa. Of course I'm upset. This is really hard, and I get really frustrated. But I'm thankful to be alive."

Linda later told their mother, "It should have been me, Mom. My kids are grown. How can she take care of anyone if she loses her hands and feet?"

"Loretta will be fine," her mother assured her. "God will give her the strength she needs, when she needs it. And we don't know yet if she'll lose her hands and feet."

Loretta went to rehab several times a week, and she worked hard to become more independent. She wanted to shave her underarms, so her therapist fashioned a loop that fit over her wrist and around an electric razor. It held the razor stable against her bandaged hand, so she could move it up and down to shave by herself. They gave her a metal button-hooker, so she could button her clothes. It took some practice, but eventually, she could stick it through the buttonhole, hook it around the button, then pull the button back through the hole. She learned to apply her own makeup by holding the brushes and pencils between her bandaged fingers, although she usually needed someone to put them there. Sometimes she used the special tubes they gave her to hold her silverware, but she found they weren't worth the effort. At home, Loretta had always paid the bills and balanced the checkbook, so why not now? Wally brought the stack of supplies to the playroom recliner and wedged the pen between the bandages, so she could write checks.

For Loretta, getting on with her life had to include exercise, which had always been a big part of her identity. Of course, getting around on her knees was an effort, and sometimes she exercised by walking across the floor on her hips, which she termed the "hiney hike." She planted her rear on the floor and took steps by rotating her hips, first one and then the other, which turned out to be great exercise for her waist, too.

Thanks to her nephew Kevin's wife, Loretta started doing leg lifts. Chrissie was adamant that Loretta shouldn't sit around any more than necessary. She convinced her that strengthening her thigh muscles would get her mobile again, so they got to work. Chrissie told her to sit up straight on the edge of her chair, and she put weights on top of Loretta's thighs, but never more than five pounds. Then she lifted her thighs up and down.

Chrissie made it fun. She'd say things like "Come on, you can give me five more, come on," like she was her personal trainer. It was a far cry from jumping on the trampoline or riding a bike like she used to do, but it was something Loretta could handle. She even took it a step further and laid down on her side in the recliner to do leg lifts.

Every few days, a visiting nurse stopped by to check on Loretta, and she thought that some of the circulation in her extremities might have returned. As portions of her arms and legs healed, the blackened skin peeled off—almost like a scab—to reveal new, pink skin underneath. The nurse even noticed some swelling in her toes. *Is swelling a good sign?* Loretta wondered. She thought it might be.

She went back to the hospital twice a week to be evaluated or to have an ultrasound of her limbs that would show if there was any circulation. Each time, the car ride was tense. So much was at stake, and Loretta prayed silently the whole way there. *Please God, let my hands and feet have better blood flow. Let there be a stronger pulse. I need my hands and feet. Please let them get better.*

After several trips, the doctor had news she didn't want to hear. "I'm sorry, but we don't see a lot of improvement in your legs," he said. "At first, we saw some healing, but now it seems to have stopped. I think it's time to amputate your legs."

"No, no! Not yet," Loretta said. Her stomach tensed, her head spun. "I'm not ready to give up." Already, the blackness had receded a few inches on each of her limbs. To her, every bit of reclaimed tissue made a big difference. Wally agreed.

The doctor suggested they amputate on the first of February, but Wally protested. "We haven't given it enough time yet," he said.

"Okay," the doctor said. "I think its fine to hold off, if that's what you want to do. There's no infection, and it's not hurting anything to wait, but I think your legs are physically finished healing. But it's just as important to prepare yourself emotionally, so if you need more time, then take it."

They appreciated his considerate response. Since the first day Loretta was wheeled into his hospital, this doctor had shown her nothing but compassionate care, and as bad as the prognosis sounded, his kind manner softened the blow.

Meanwhile, Loretta tried to learn something new every day that would make her more self-sufficient. In some respects, the days seemed to drag by, but in other ways, the time flew. Before she knew it, it was Valentine's Day. Loretta had grieved that she could no longer wear her wedding rings, and to celebrate the holiday, Wally bought her a gold chain. He threaded her rings through the chain and put it around her neck.

"Wally, this is beautiful," Loretta said. "Thank you."

"Now you can wear them even closer to your heart," he said.

After another week and a few more trips to the doctor, Loretta finally accepted the inevitable. No new skin grew under the dead tissue, and deep down, she knew the healing process was over.

She had been getting around the house remarkably well, but her petrified feet were heavy, like dead weight that she dragged behind her. Her toes had hardened, and they clicked like marbles on the tile floor. The skin on the bottoms of her feet was completely black, and there was no other tissue that could be grafted onto them, none that was considered "load bearing" or strong enough to use on the balls of her feet. She knew it was time to amputate.

"I think this is it," she told Wally. "My feet are holding me back now. They feel like anchors holding me down. I want to go ahead with the surgery, so I can get new legs and walk again. I need to get my life back."

The surgery was scheduled for February 22, when both of her legs would be amputated, eight inches below the knee.

Though she was losing her legs, at the same time, Loretta had no doubt that many of her prayers had been answered during the past few weeks. Her legs had partially healed, and both her arms had more circulation than they had at first. When she had been discharged from the hospital, they thought they would have to amputate her legs directly below her knees. But because of the extra healing time, those plans had changed.

"There's been significant improvement in your circulation," her doctor said, "and you've regained several inches of healthy tissue in each of your limbs." The circulation in her legs had actually progressed down past her ankles. "And yet, I think it's best to amputate several inches above the point where the circulation stops," he said.

"Why would we do that?" Loretta cried out. "We prayed for every single bit of pink skin and for all of this circulation. Why would I let you take that part, too?"

"Because in the long run, it will allow you to have better control of your prosthetic limbs and will actually help you to walk better," he said. "When you remove the foot at the joint, it's called a Symes amputation. If I did that, I believe it would be much more difficult for you to get back to your daily activities using prosthetics."

Loretta cried and cried, grieving over the healthy tissue she would lose. "This is awful," she told Wally. "He says it will help me to walk better later, but it seems like they're taking more than they should." It was another emotional blow she had to absorb.

The decision was made, and it was time to tell Mitch and Alyssa that their mother's legs were coming off. Together, Wally and Loretta told them about the upcoming operation, and they both seemed to accept it at the time, but they later asked their dad some questions when they were alone.

"I know you explained it to us Dad, but I just don't understand why they have to take her legs," Mitch said.

"I know," Wally said. "It is hard to understand, but the medicine that saved Mom's life also caused her hands and feet to die."

"Her hands? Are they taking her hands, too?" Mitch asked, alarmed. His mother's hands had been bandaged, and now he wondered if they would be cut off, too. Loretta had never allowed her children to see them unwrapped, never allowed them to see the petrified tissue and her witch-green fingernails.

"They're not doing anything to her hands right now," Wally told him. "We'll have to wait and see how they heal." He didn't want the kids to know more than they needed to at this point. It was better to take one step at a time.

Mitch and Alyssa weren't the only ones who needed to know about her surgery. Their family and friends needed to be told as well, and Wally thought Loretta ought to be the one to tell them.

"I don't even want to say that word—amputation," Loretta told him, shaking her head. "It's such an *ugly* word."

"Maybe if you say it out loud, it will help you take ownership of it," Wally said. "It might help you start to accept it."

The night before her surgery, the family gathered together for dinner— Loretta, Wally, both sets of their parents, her sister Laura, and Mitch and Alyssa. They tried to take Loretta's mind off the surgery, but of course, it was all anyone could think about, especially Loretta. The grandmothers prepared the meal and, for the first time ever, they ate dinner in their formal dining room.

Loretta had spent a lot of time and energy decorating each room in their house, tackling one room every year. After almost nine years, the dining room was the last one on the list. She had been happy that it would be finished before

Christmas and had bought the light fixture and the furniture, and all the fabrics for the window treatments just a week or two before she hit her hand.

As she sat at the table, she thought back a few weeks to when the wallpaper was hung. Jim, her paperhanger, was sitting on his ladder, cutting the paper to cover the cold air return when the doorbell rang. It was Norm, delivering a package that contained a pair of denim shorts and some sandals she'd ordered. She ran upstairs, closed her bedroom door, and tried them on. Loretta had worked hard to get in shape. She rode the exercise bike and jumped on the trampoline, and her hard work paid off. She looked fabulous. *It's only December, but I can't wait to wear these,* she thought.

But she never got to wear those shorts or the sandals. She never even put them on again. And she never did get to entertain in her new dining room. The only time she sat at that table was the night before she lost her legs.

When they finished eating, Loretta asked if Laura would help her with something. She wanted to shave her legs one last time. If she was having surgery, she was going in clean and smooth. She wanted to muster as much dignity as she could under the circumstances.

She got in the tub and propped her feet over the side while Laura ran the water. She still didn't want to get her hands and feet wet because the doctors had been so adamant that they stay dry during the healing process. Laura shook the can of shaving cream, sprayed the foam into her hand, and gently spread it over Loretta's upper legs, the part that was still healthy. Laura was careful not to nick her skin as she slid the razor over the foam, but both of them were preoccupied; neither was thinking about shaving. Laura lost track of what she was doing and kept shaving the same part of Loretta's leg—at least five times.

"What am I doing?" Laura laughed.

"I was wondering how many times you were going to shave that area," Loretta said. "I thought my leg must be really hairy," she added, trying to lighten the moment.

The girls laughed and goofed off, blew bubbles in each other's faces, and steamed up the mirror. For a few minutes, they were lighthearted. Loretta got out of the tub and stood on her knees while Laura helped her dry off and get dressed, then went into the bedroom. When she got to the side of her bed, she leaned against the mattress, dropped her head down, and started to wail—a grief-stricken keening that filled the room.

This cannot be happening to me! Loretta thought. *How can I get up in the morning and go to the hospital to have my legs AMPUTATED?*

Laura tried to comfort her, but it wasn't possible, so she held her tight and cried with her. After a while, Loretta said she needed some time alone.

God, please be with me tomorrow, she prayed over and over until Wally came upstairs. He picked her up, put her in bed, and put on the fuzzy socks she wore to hide her feet—one last time.

Over the past weeks, Loretta had come to a gradual acceptance of her fate, but it wasn't complete. She was so tired of being on her knees and wanted to stand up and walk, and the only way she could do that was if she got rid of her dead limbs. In her head, she knew the circulation wasn't coming back—but in her heart, it was agonizing.

After Wally put her in bed, she cried a little more, but as she talked to God, she made her final peace with the surgery.

That night, her sleep was sound.

Chapter 14

Morning came, and it was finally time to leave. Loretta crawled down the stairs on her knees, ready to face her future. Laura, Wanda, and Wally were taking her to the hospital, while Wally's parents and Charles stayed at the house. Tears streamed down her father's anguished face as he said goodbye to his daughter. "I'm praying for you, and I love you," he told her.

Wally's mother echoed those words, and then her father-in-law laid his big hands on either side of her face and whispered, "I like lemonade." Loretta was puzzled. His comment seemed to come out of nowhere, but after a moment, she understood what he meant: If life gives you lemons, what do you make?

They arrived a little early, and while they waited for the surgeon, the nurse asked her to take everything off and put on the hospital gown. She was still wearing her fuzzy socks, so Wally pulled them off. They all stared. The night before, her feet were black, but they had been plump. This morning they were completely concave, shriveled up like dried fruit, skin over bone. For the second time, she felt like a character from the *Wizard of Oz*, like Dorothy's house had landed and her feet had shriveled up.

Loretta now had closure. She would never look back and wonder if she should have waited longer. Her feet were dead, and it was time to move on.

When the surgeon came in, Loretta joked, "Make sure I'm straight in bed, then measure twice and cut once." She teased about drawing tick marks on her legs, mainly to lighten the mood for everyone else in the room, but she really wasn't feeling all that funny.

It was time to part. She kissed Wally, her mother, and Laura goodbye. As they wheeled her into the operating room, she looked back and saw Wally sobbing, his whole body heaving. Her mother stepped over and wrapped her arms around him.

It was a long, painful wait. Many prayers were spoken, and many tears were shed. The surgery lasted longer than expected, making the time even more grueling. In the waiting room, a total stranger who had heard about Loretta came up to Laura and said, "I've been praying for you and your family." That simple, kind gesture reassured and uplifted them.

Even so, Wally was in anguish. *After all this time and everything she's been through,* he thought, *here it is—they take her away. They're chipping away at her.* Being powerless was foreign to him. He'd been in charge his whole life. Wally took care of situations, was a problem solver. But this time, he could do nothing. *She's alive, but what she has to endure is so horrible. Will she ever walk again?*

At last, the surgery was over. Loretta woke up with both legs casted, and she was in tremendous pain. "It hurts," she told Wally, "I need a rawhide bone to bite down on!"

Wally's eyes widened, and he turned to the nurse, "What are you giving her for pain?"

"She's getting morphine, but we can't give her any more yet. It's not time."

"Morphine—she doesn't respond to morphine! It does nothing for her pain—she needs Dilaudid. We discovered that when she was in the hospital before."

So they switched her medication, and her pain eased. The drug was administered on demand by pushing a button whenever it was needed. But once again, Loretta couldn't use her hands, so she couldn't do it herself. Wanda and Laura stayed overnight, and Wally went home to be with the kids. They took turns sleeping, so they could push the button for Loretta, but it was mainly Laura who monitored her sister. She insisted that their mother get some sleep—she was both physically and emotionally exhausted from the last couple of months. Laura measured the night in ten-minute increments, releasing the painkiller to keep Loretta as comfortable as possible.

The next morning, Wanda and Laura went down to the cafeteria for an early breakfast. They were worried that when Loretta woke up, she would be morose and depressed, and they wanted to eat quickly and get back to her room before she woke up.

But Loretta opened her eyes before they got back. Alone in her bed, it was her moment of truth. She had always been tall—around 5'10"—and before the amputations, her body looked long under the sheets. Now the sheets were tucked tight around her, and she didn't recognize her shape. Each leg was twelve inches shorter. Her long legs were really gone.

Rather than panic, she reminded herself that if she wanted to move forward with her life, this is what had to happen. She had to get rid of those dead legs. Now it was time to figure out the next step. To her, that meant she needed to gain strength, and when Wanda and Laura got back to her room, Loretta was in bed doing leg lifts. It was her first step in reclaiming her life.

Over the next few days, Loretta found that she had not only lost her legs, but she was also losing her hair. It clung to her pillowcase in clumps, which upset her because her hair had always been important to her—as it is to nearly every woman. It had started falling out when she was in the hospital the first time, and her new medications accelerated the loss. For the time being, it was one more thing she would have to live without.

She didn't linger in the hospital for long. Her legs were amputated on Friday, and on Tuesday they wheeled her from the hospital to the adjoining rehab facility. Loretta was assigned to a prosthetist, a person skilled and certified in making, fitting, and servicing prosthetics. He counseled her about her future limbs and the rehabilitation process and made fiberglass casts to protect what was left of her legs. He didn't want her to hit the bones on anything—especially the smaller, more fragile tibia that could be quite painful if it got bumped or rubbed.

"You'll be with us for two weeks," the doctor told her, "while you recuperate and learn to adapt."

Loretta fought back tears, but said matter-of-factly, "No, Wally is off on Thursday, and that's when I'm going home."

Loretta had already been in the hospital for over a month when she was sick, and for an additional few days after the surgery. She had only been at home for five weeks in between, and the thought of being stuck in a hospital environment for another two weeks felt like a prison sentence.

She was determined to get out of there, but the doctor only said, "We'll see." He had no idea what she'd already accomplished during the past five weeks, and he didn't understand that she was not their typical amputee who had suddenly lost her legs. Loretta had already learned how to get around, and she was certain she could prove that she was ready to be released.

It was all about being safe. She had to demonstrate that she could get in and out of a car, in and out of the bathtub, up and off a toilet, and up and down the stairs. The doctor was surprised when she passed all the necessary tests, and he let her go home two days later—on Thursday—just like she said she would.

Mitch and Alyssa were waiting with Wanda, the current grandmother-in-residence. Wally wheeled her inside, and Loretta saw her children look first at her short legs and then at her face, trying to gauge how she was accepting her new situation. "We're home!" Loretta announced and held out her arms for a hug. Tears welled in her eyes, but she did not cry. She was determined to be strong for her children.

They ran to give her a hug, which added to Loretta's confidence that everything would somehow work out. For the next few weeks, she dealt with the healing process, which was not easy by any means, and the rest of the family went back to their normal routines. Life goes on, even when it changes.

Though she was suffering physically and emotionally, Loretta never suffered from lack of love. Friends and acquaintances brought her gifts of comfort, small and large. One of Mitch's schoolmates lived in a nearby neighborhood, and his mother stopped by.

"I thought this blanket might be something you could use while you're healing," she said. "Would you like me to lay it across your lap?"

"Yes, but there's something written on it," Loretta said. "What does it say?"

"It's a poem. That's the reason I got it. This is what I've been praying for you." She read the verse aloud to Loretta:

I said a prayer for you today and know God must have heard;
I felt the answer in my heart although He spoke no word.
I didn't ask for wealth or fame. I knew you wouldn't mind.
I asked Him to send treasures of a far more lasting kind.
I asked that He'd be near you at the start of each new day,
To grant you health and blessings and friends to share the way.

"Thank you," Loretta whispered. "I love it."

Loretta had grown used to walking around the house on her knees, but it was a completely different experience after the amputations. When she still had her legs, they counter-balanced the weight of her torso, but now she didn't have the weight of her feet to anchor her from behind. She needed to find a new point of balance, so she wouldn't pitch forward and land on her face, which could easily happen since she couldn't use her hands to break a fall.

It took a couple of days to figure it out, and by then she insisted on returning to her normal routines, which included being ready to greet her children when they got home from school. Every day by three o'clock, one of the grandmothers helped her get cleaned up, and she put on a little makeup, did her hair, and had a snack ready for the kids like she always had.

One day, she wanted more than a home shampoo. She was ready to get out of the house, and Wally volunteered to take her to the hair salon. The wheelchair was new to them both, and as Wally pushed her toward the salon, they came to a steep curb. Instead of easing the wheelchair down on its back wheels, he pushed her forward on the front wheels—and she started to slide out. Normally, a person would stick their foot out to stop the slide, but Loretta didn't have feet. And she couldn't grab the chair arms because her hands were bandaged, so she just kept sliding forward.

When he realized his mistake, Wally jerked the chair upright before she actually fell out, and the whole situation struck them both as hysterically funny. They laughed heartily, able to find the humor in a distressing situation.

"You were trying to ditch me!" Loretta accused, laughing at their predicament.

Over the next month, Loretta had a series of appointments to be fitted for her first prosthetic legs, which had three main parts: *the interface, the components,* and *the cover.*

The *interface* is where the artificial limb attaches to the body, and it consists of a socket and a rigid frame. The socket is usually made of plastic or a laminated material and is where the functional parts of the prosthesis—or the components—attach to the person. The frame, which is made of graphite or similar materials, provides structural support around the socket. Before attaching the leg, the patient pulls on a separate liner made of silicone or soft polyurethane to cushion the natural leg and provide a tight fit.

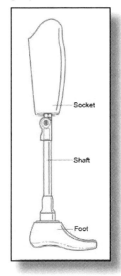

The *components* are the functional parts of the prosthesis, and they include metal shafts that serve as bones, as well as the feet, ankles, and toes. Some people who wear a prosthesis don't mind having the components exposed, but others want to have them concealed by a *cover*. The prosthetist shapes the cover from foam or another material such as silicone, and it may or may not look lifelike, depending on whether the cover is custom designed or off-the-shelf.

Before Loretta went in for her first fitting, Wally ran across a newspaper ad that featured Heather Mills, who was a fashion model at the time and a single-leg amputee. Both her legs were beautiful. Coincidentally, Loretta happened to be watching *The View* one morning when Heather was a guest. She talked about her new book, *Out on a Limb,* so when Wally mentioned that he'd seen Heather in an ad, Loretta said, "And, I saw her on television talking about life as an amputee."

At the time, Heather was the ambassador for the global Adopt-A-Minefield campaign, and she was engaged to Paul McCartney. She had started her work with amputees in 1991. Two years later and long before she met Paul, she was hit by a police motorcycle in London and suffered multiple injuries that included a broken pelvis, and her left leg was severed below the knee. Heather now represented the organization as an amputee herself.

Wally showed Loretta the ad, and she was amazed at how beautiful Heather's prosthetic leg looked. It was encouraging, not only for Loretta, but for Mitch and Alyssa, too, because it helped them picture what their mother's legs could eventually look like.

Wally did some research and printed out information about Dorset Orthopaedic Co. Ltd. in England, the clinic that built Heather's prosthetic leg. Loretta wanted her legs to look natural, to be beautiful like Heather's leg was, so they took the ad and the information to her first fitting.

Immediately, her hopes were dashed. The head of the prosthetics unit told

Loretta that the photograph was not real, that it had been staged. "That's not the direction you should pursue," he said. "You're never going to wear high heels again."

They took Loretta's measurements and made molds of her residual limbs, and when the day finally came to get her new legs, Loretta was excited, even though she had no idea what they would look like. It was now the third week in March, and she had not stood upright in three months, not since December 16, the day she first went to the hospital. Getting her legs was the next step to finding her "new normal," and she couldn't wait to walk out on her own two feet.

But when they brought the legs out, Loretta felt sick. They were nothing like she expected. How could she ever wear these? They were fat and plastic looking, like something you'd see on a cheap doll in a discount store. And the color was all wrong. When she had her fittings, they told her to "choose a tan," like she was picking out pantyhose instead of a color she'd be wearing every day, and these didn't even come close to matching her skin tone. The feet were so flat and big that all she'd be able to wear were tennis shoes, and Loretta *never* wore tennis shoes, not unless she was working out. She always wore heels. Like a curse, the prosthetist's words rung in her ears. *"You'll never wear heels again."*

Her prosthetist put the legs on and wheeled her over to a stanchion where she was supposed to try to walk. She couldn't use her hands to stabilize herself—which is what the rails were for—so the therapists walked alongside her. The first time she stood up, Loretta nearly blacked out from the pain. Standing on the ends of her sawed-off bones, the tender tips bore all of her body weight and pressed into the hard plastic of the massive legs.

It wasn't supposed to hurt like this, but Loretta didn't know that. She didn't know that the legs didn't feel right because the swelling in her natural legs had gone down in the weeks between the time they had taken her measurements and when the liners and sockets were actually created. She assumed that this was her fate, that she would be stuck with these horrendous, plastic bubble-legs that made her shudder in pain with every step.

That morning, Loretta had been so full of joy, so expectant that this would be her turning point, that today she would start walking again and would resume her life, and with a little practice, she'd become self-sufficient and independent again. She knew her kids were thinking "Mom's getting new legs, she's going to be her old self soon." But that didn't happen. She couldn't even walk across the room, much less out the door.

They went back and forth to the rehab center multiple times, trying to get her legs to fit right. Over the coming months, Loretta had to have half a dozen or more sets of legs because her natural legs were still changing. The prosthetics did get smaller over time, but the feet never changed. They always installed those same big, flat feet—every single time.

Eventually, the prosthetists achieved a better fit, and Loretta had regular therapy appointments so she could learn how to use them. Her therapist strapped a safety harness around her waist and scattered cones around the room, and she had to lean over and pick them up. Wearing the legs was like being on stilts, and it made her very nervous to walk. It was a different world to her now, and things she had never noticed before now became major obstacles. Stepping up or down a curb was especially frightening, and she avoided it at all costs.

Sometimes the prosthetics felt too tight, and her legs were so painful that she could feel her pulse throb in them. She often went outside in the freezing cold, hoping the temperature would shrink what was left of her legs. She reasoned that in the winter, her rings slid right off her fingers because the cold reduced any swelling, so she went outside and prayed that her legs would shrink, so her prosthetics would fit better.

The day Loretta received her first legs was, indeed, a turning point, but not how she expected. Until then, she had always been positive, even if it was only for the benefit of others, and she always found the bright spot in any situation, no matter what was going on. But wearing those ugly legs wore her down. She felt diminished, embarrassed—even shamed. She'd worked hard her entire life to maintain an attractive appearance, and now that seemed totally out of reach. She would never feel beautiful looking like this. Plus, the pain was so horrendous that she didn't even want to put the legs on, and she was supposed to wear them all day. Even when she was sitting in the wheelchair, she had to have the legs on.

It was too much. Loretta was ready to throw in the towel.

Chapter 15

All this time, Loretta was still going for debrisment to remove the dead layers of skin on her hands, and for a while, they uncovered fresh skin underneath, but it finally reached the point where her hands were no longer healing. They were dead—black and hard—with no fresh skin whatsoever. Her fingers had curled like claws. She found it odd that a part of her body could still be attached, yet be so obviously dead. It was like the blood vessels that went down her arm did a complete u-turn when they got to her wrists, like they'd come to a bad neighborhood and turned around right in the middle of the street. Without that supply of blood, the tissue died.

On April 23, Loretta was back in surgery. She checked into the outpatient center, and the surgeon removed three fingers on her right hand and amputated her index finger down to the second joint, leaving only the section below that knuckle. Ironically, her right thumb remained fully intact, a bizarre twist because that was the spot where she had hit her hand on the banister, the very point where the initial strep infection had entered her body. The surgeon bandaged her up and gave her an antibiotic, and although she was in pain for a while, she was relieved to have this step behind her.

She gradually regained use of that hand, but in an altogether different way. Always the optimist, Loretta found the bright spot. "Never underestimate the power of a thumb and forefinger!" she quipped. Her right thumb and what was left of her index finger in many ways became her salvation. She used them for everything—to hold cooking utensils, to apply her makeup, to comb her hair, to hold a washcloth, to write, and just about everything else.

And yet, her ordeal wasn't over. On July 18, her left hand—not just the fingers, but the entire hand—was amputated. The black mass at the end of her arm was dead, and she knew it was time to let it go, too. It was another devastating loss. They amputated in front of her wrist bone, leaving the joint intact to give her better control after it healed.

Lying on the operating table, she felt so vulnerable, so minimized, so pruned. They'd taken her legs, part of her right hand, and now she was losing her left hand. To top it off, she'd lost most of her hair, too.

Of all her amputations, this one was the worst. Loretta's hands played a huge role in how she expressed herself—to stroke a child's hair, to give a loving squeeze, to emphasize an exciting story, to scratch a back. She had always admired other women's pretty hands and well-groomed nails, and she noticed them now more than ever.

They amputated on a Thursday, and on Friday she went back to the doctor for a follow-up visit. This surgery was so much worse than all the others. When she lost her legs, she'd been mentally prepared, but she knew she would walk again. And losing the fingers on her right hand wasn't so bad because afterward, it still looked like her hand, except that her fingers weren't as long. This was completely different.

The nurse unspooled the gauze until what was left of her hand was fully exposed. It didn't even look like a hand. It was a swollen, bloody ball, black from the bruises and outlined with ugly stitching that would look more at home on a baseball than on a body.

Loretta screamed. "I don't know if I can take anymore!" she cried. Wally pulled her into his arms and wept with her.

"I'll never be able to wear my wedding rings again." She'd been wearing her rings on the gold chain that Wally had given her, but to her, it was a temporary solution. She always hoped that her hand would heal, and her rings would return to their rightful place. That would never happen now.

The surgeon understood their distress, and he called them at home later that day. "I have resources if you want to go to counseling," he offered.

"But we didn't go," Loretta said. "Our lives were already so full of doctor appointments and rehab sessions and everything else related to my care, that we just didn't have the energy to fit in one more thing. We didn't go, and that was the only time anyone suggested counseling of any kind."

Slowly, Loretta recuperated and took charge of what she could. She vowed that she wouldn't be what she called "Loretta in the Rough" for long and focused on getting well for the sake of her family. She was determined to take care of Wally, Mitch, and Alyssa, which had been her main motivation all along, so she prayed for God's blessings and asked for his help, which was the only way she found comfort during those dark times. Somehow she had to find decent prosthetics—for both her hands and her legs—that would make her feel attractive again. She had to find comfortable legs, so she could walk and get on with her life.

Meanwhile, the bills poured in. Wally spread them all over their queen-sized bed, and the papers covered the entire surface. He matched the endless invoices with their associated payments from the insurance company, and tried to figure out how much they owed themselves.

They were constantly being billed for something, and the insurance company fought them at every turn. Loretta would sit on her knees on the floor, unable to see what was up on the bed, but she knew it was completely covered with bills—from the hospitals, the doctors, and the pharmacies, in addition to all Explanation of Benefits forms from the insurance company.

Wally tried to coordinate it all. "Okay, this goes with that one, and they're going to pay that, but why did they deny this one? I gotta call about that one."

The unpaid bills represented much more than financial pressure to Loretta. Before she got sick, they had vacationed at the beach at Hilton Head, South Carolina, and had fallen in love with the area. They had been careful with their money their entire marriage and had always saved up for what they wanted until they could afford it. Now that their house was fully decorated, they were on to the next goal—purchasing a vacation home in Hilton Head.

But that would never happen now. Not with all these medical bills. It would take all their resources to dig out of this pile. And who was the cause of it?

We won't get to Hilton Head because of me. It's my fault.

Loretta felt like she was a problem, just another bill and a financial burden that Wally had to deal with, and every time he said they couldn't do this or that because she might need new legs, she felt like she'd been stabbed. For the first time in her life, her inner self was in crisis. She felt completely diminished, particularly in terms of her marriage. *Wally has to change his whole schedule to haul me to hospitals and doctor appointments, and he has to juggle all these bills and keep everyone going. I have nothing to give back to him.* **Nothing.** *And what if I can't ever give back? I'm not a partner anymore—I'm just another bill.*

During the next year, Loretta was almost always in pain, at first from the surgeries, and then from her prosthetics, which still hurt so much that she couldn't wear them for any real length of time. She broke out in a sweat when she tried to walk, and usually ended up with diarrhea, which is how her body responded to the intense pain. Her therapist suggested they try something to pinpoint the problem. Loretta was feeling pressure on her legs where there shouldn't be, and as strange as it may sound, her therapist put a ball of Silly Putty inside the sockets where her legs rested. After she walked a few steps, her legs made an impression in the putty that showed the points of irritation. With that knowledge, they tried to make the necessary adjustments.

Even so, the legs still didn't feel great, and the friction between her natural leg and the prosthetic rubbed her raw. She had to pay close attention to her calendar, so she could manage her "leg time." Since she only had a few good steps every day, she had to choose them wisely. If she knew she'd be taking Alyssa to dance, she wouldn't run the vacuum or go to the grocery store and, instead, would do low-key things that didn't involve any wear and tear on her legs. If she walked for long periods, the pain was often so intense that it traveled all the way up her lower back, and she would have to hobble in and out of stores, hurrying through her errands, so she could get back home and have someone help her take them off.

Sometimes Wally had to take her legs off in the strangest places, simply because she couldn't stand the pain—in church, while they were driving down the road—wherever. They always tried to be discreet, but pain was her constant companion, and it dogged her every step.

One evening, they took Mitch and Alyssa out to a nice restaurant, a favorite place that had long, white tablecloths and linen napkins folded into swans. The hostess seated them, and while they perused their menus, Loretta shifted in her seat. She shifted again. Soon she was rocking in her chair.

"What's wrong?" Wally asked.

"The same as always. It's my legs. They're killing me."

"Do you need to take them off?" Wally asked, and he removed them for her. Now what were they supposed to do with an errant set of legs in a fancy restaurant? Wally shot the kids a devious look and slid them under the tablecloth, upright, with the toes pointing out. Whenever someone walked by and saw those feet, clearly unattached to a body, they reacted. Some stared just a moment too long to be polite, and others looked once, then looked again, completely incapable of processing the sight. Every time, the whole family erupted in laughter.

———

Throughout her ordeal, the prayers for Loretta's recovery reached far and wide, across the country, across the ocean, and to people from all walks of life. Her friends and family members called their friends and family members, who reached out to their own circle of friends, and so on. It seemed that everyone was praying for Loretta. One of her friends from church had even emailed Heather Mills and asked her to pray for Loretta. She knew that Heather was known for helping other amputees and remembered that Loretta had seen her on *The View*. She found Heather's email address on her website and, on a whim, she sent her a note. She was more than surprised when Heather wrote back to ask about Loretta's condition.

When Heather learned that Loretta had just been fitted for her prosthetic legs and was having a terrible time, she asked for her phone number.

Chapter 16

The night Loretta got home from her first, failed attempt at walking on those ugly, agonizing bubble-legs, she was defeated. She'd met her match and had lost the battle. That morning, she had been so hopeful that this would be her turning point and that she could start to reclaim her life. Instead, she was almost ready to give up.

The next morning, her misery was compounded when the insurance company called to say that her prosthetic legs might not be covered by her policy. Even though the legs had already been manufactured, she might not get to have them after all.

Loretta sat on the kitchen floor and cried to her mom. "I can't believe they would deny me my legs! This has been one thing after another, and I'm so sick of it! Even though they're ugly and painful, I have to have legs, and we can't afford them without the insurance money."

She went back upstairs and fumed in the playroom recliner, her blanket on her lap. Absorbed in her pain and frustration, she wasn't too happy about answering the phone when it rang. She figured it was the insurance company calling back to give her more grief, but she picked it up anyway and heard a voice with a distinct British accent.

"Hi, this is Heather Mills, how are you doing?"

Needless to say, Loretta was shocked, but Heather had such a way about her that right from the start, it seemed like they were old friends. They were on the phone for forty-five minutes, and even though Heather was a celebrity and was engaged to Paul McCartney, Loretta wasn't the least bit star-struck.

Talking to Heather was like talking to a girlfriend. And what did they talk about? Loretta complained about her hair falling out.

"Don't stress the small stuff," Heather told her. "Many celebrities wear wigs just to give their hair a break from the styling. Just put some conditioner on it and wear a wig."

Loretta poured her whole heart out to Heather. She told her how awful her legs looked, and that she was afraid that she wouldn't ever be able to walk with them. "And I don't think I'll ever feel pretty or feminine again." Loretta opened up to her about things she hadn't even told her family. Heather, like no one else, understood and was able to offer her insight and credible advice about moving on after an amputation, simply because she had done it herself.

"Paul and I are coming to Chicago," Heather said. "I'd love it if you would come to our hotel, so I can meet you and talk to you in person."

Loretta was ecstatic. Of course she wanted to meet Heather, and it gave her something to look forward to. Her phone calls with friends turned into, "Oh my gosh, you're never going to believe who called me!" instead of the dry old, "What's going on, and how are you feeling?" It was something fresh and fun, and it made her feel hopeful again.

That phone call from Heather changed her entire outlook. Loretta couldn't believe that someone like Heather would take time out of her busy lifestyle to reach out to her. She felt like a million bucks. She didn't know any other amputees at that point, so she had no one to talk to, no one to lead the way. It was obvious that even though Heather had lost a leg, she was still loving her life and going about being beautiful, and she was about to be married to Paul McCartney.

From that point forward, Loretta put her renewed energy into her physical therapy, began to regain her strength, and pushed herself to do as much as possible.

Meanwhile, Loretta did what Heather had suggested and bought herself a wig—but she felt embarrassed to wear it. She thought it made her look like Sandra Dee. It had swooped bangs, and she had to wear a headband with it to hold it off her face. It was better than her own scant hair, but still, it was yet another reminder of how much of herself and her individual style she had lost.

She got up early on the day she was going to meet Heather, and while she was getting ready, Loretta sat on the floor of her closet in front of the mirror. Her mother handed her various makeup items and wedged the brushes between her bandages.

"This is a big day for you," Wanda said. "It's so exciting!"

Loretta didn't respond. Her eyes flooded. Of course this was a big day, but it wasn't what she truly wanted. She looked in the mirror at her mother's reflection and said, "I'd rather have my old life back and be getting ready to go to Target."

They both burst into tears.

Later that morning, Wally wheeled Loretta into the Ritz-Carlton in her black skirt and black top, wearing that terrible hair and those ugly, ugly legs. She was about to meet a fashion model, but there was no feeling cute that day, not for Loretta. Wally wheeled her to a couch, and Heather immediately walked across the room and sat down next to her. She introduced herself, and it was 'kiss, kiss' on both cheeks in the typical British fashion.

"Could you show me your leg?" Loretta asked.

Heather propped it up on the coffee table and pulled up her pant leg— and then someone came out of the woodwork and snapped a photo. Heather's bodyguard, Missy, stepped in.

"I'm sorry but this is a private meeting. Could you please move back?" she said.

"Better yet, let's go up to my room," Heather suggested.

When they got upstairs, they both popped off their legs to get a good look. Heather showed Loretta and Wally how her own leg fit and how nice it looked. She agreed that Loretta's legs were pathetic and assured her that there was nothing vain about wanting to have natural-looking legs.

Loretta was excited to know that, eventually, she might be able to have such beautiful legs, but she was also aggravated that she'd have to go all the way to England to get them. She didn't know that high-quality prosthetics were available in the U.S. because she'd never looked for them. She simply followed the recommendations of those who were treating her and didn't look any further.

And now that she saw the type of the leg she wanted and knew where to get them, Loretta was sold—except for one important factor. How much would they cost? Wally had worked out their issues with the insurance company, but there was a limit to what they would pay. *Okay, you are who you are,* Loretta thought, *and you're engaged to Paul McCartney and can afford the best of the best. But what about me?*

"Do you mind telling me what you paid for your leg?" she asked.

Heather told them what her leg cost, and they were shocked. It was almost the same price they'd paid for one of Loretta's legs and was within their reach.

"I've never wanted to go out of the country, Wally, but guess what?" Loretta said. "We're going to England!"

Heather had several appointments throughout that day, and anyone who was scheduled to meet with her came to the Ritz. She had an interview with Disney Channel Radio that afternoon and asked if Loretta would like to participate. They went to a room where the equipment and microphones were already set up, and Heather spoke about her role as ambassador for Adopt-a-Minefield and how all amputees deserved to have good prosthetic limbs. Then she incorporated Loretta into the interview.

"I just met this woman and she's an incredible person, and I want you to hear her story," she said. The Disney crew hadn't planned to interview Loretta, but they asked her all kinds of questions about what happened to her, and she told her full story. Afterward, she looked over to the other side of the room where Wally and Missy were waiting. They were both crying. Even though Wally had been through everything with her and experienced it when she did, he was openly weeping, feeling the pain all over again.

After the interview, Heather received an award from the Rehabilitation Institute of Chicago for her charity work. Loretta sat nearby in her wheelchair, and Heather was fired up and kept saying to them, "There is no reason why this woman should have to wear legs that look like this!" She insisted that they examine the difference between her leg and the clunky legs that Loretta wore. She hiked up Loretta's skirt, and it flashed a bit too high above her knees, but Heather brushed it off. "Loretta doesn't mind," she said. "She has great thighs—I've seen them!"

When it was time for Loretta and Wally to leave, it was 'kiss-kiss' again, and Loretta was flying high on the drive back home. Being with Heather had been easy, and Loretta felt certain that God had specifically sent her, so she would have real hope again. Heather hadn't let her amputation stop her or even slow her down. She was glamorous and happy and was living a full life, which is exactly what Loretta wanted to do.

Sir Paul McCartney and Heather Mills were married that June, and in September, they were back in Chicago for Paul's concert at the United Center, which was part of his world tour. Heather's sister, Fiona, was managing her schedule, and she called Loretta to invite her to be a guest.

Loretta and Wally were already in Chicago at the Drake Hotel with Dr. Jean Pillet, the prosthetist from Paris who was making her left hand. Dr. Pillet traveled to about six different cities in the United States, and Chicago was one of them. At her previous appointment, they'd made a mold for the prosthetic from what remained of her right hand and matched the fingers to some that looked similar to her own. At this appointment they were painting the hand, so it would match her own skin. When it was finished, the hand would pull on like a glove.

When Fiona called, Loretta was with one of the technicians. "Is this Loretta Goebel?" an unfamiliar British voice asked.

"Yes, who is this?"

"I'm Heather's sister, Fiona. She asked me to ring you up to invite you to Paul's concert tomorrow. Would you and Wally like to come?"

After that call, Loretta could not sit still for the technician—she was far too excited. She was thrilled about the invitation, but also a little uneasy about going to the concert. She would have to navigate the crowd, climb the stairs, and deal with all the commotion, and her legs still didn't fit right. They were very painful again because they were too loose, which caused an altogether different problem. Every so often, an air pocket would erupt and make a loud and embarrassing sound, like she was passing gas. How could she meet Paul McCartney like that? Thankfully, her rehab facility was also in Chicago, so she called her prosthetist. She asked if he could meet Wally and her at the Drake Hotel and bring some filler to close up the gaps.

They met him in the lobby, and when they got in the elevator to go upstairs, there was already a man in it. When they stepped in, Loretta's leg let out a loud PFFFFFFFFFFFFTTT! Wally and the prosthetist started cracking up. It was obvious that the noise came from Loretta, and they knew exactly what the other guy must be thinking. There was no way Loretta could explain that the noise came from her leg, because who would believe that? She tried to stifle it, but by the time the man got off, they were all laughing so hard they were crying.

The prosthetist made some adjustments and solved the problem, and then Loretta faced her next dilemma: What would she wear to meet Paul McCartney? This was a once-in-a-lifetime opportunity, and she would normally have treated herself to a stylish new outfit, but she couldn't go shopping now. Their medical expenses were already so high, and even if they could afford it, she could never make her way around Michigan Avenue on those clunky legs. She didn't really have a choice. They were in Chicago for medical meetings, not a social event. She would have to wear whatever she'd brought with her, including the ugly legs and her new wig that she thought looked a lot like Barbie hair. And besides, what difference did it make what she wore? She would never feel glamorous looking like this.

The next night, they took a taxi to the performers' entrance at the United Center, where they met up with Heather and Missy, her bodyguard. Down in the bowels of the huge building, Loretta and Wally were asked to wait in a room that was already full of people, people who were the 'Who's Who' of Paul McCartney and the Beatles. They sat and listened while everyone else reminisced about when the Beatles got started and when they did this and that. *Is this really happening? Are we really with these people?* she thought. Neither Wally nor Loretta had anything to contribute to the conversation, and it was intimidating. This room, this scene, was not about Heather. This went way beyond Heather. Now they were in Paul's world, an iconic world with all kinds of hoopla and everyone running around backstage. It was wild. Surreal. Loretta couldn't have felt more out of place.

Heather popped in and said she wanted to interview Loretta for a documentary that she was producing, but this was news to Loretta. She had no idea an interview was on the agenda. Her heart jumped to her throat. They moved to a room equipped with a camera and a huge microphone that hung directly over her head. The interviewer asked her a few questions, and then Heather joined in. Some of that footage was later shown on *Larry King Live* when Heather was a guest.

That whole night was a disturbing mixture of thoughts that played in Loretta's mind. *What am I doing here? If I hadn't hit my hand I wouldn't be here ... but I'd rather not be here if I could have my life back again ... I don't know what I'm doing here ... What's the purpose of all this?*

After the concert, Paul swept through, and Heather introduced him to

Loretta and Wally. He was all sweaty and pumped up from the excitement of the audience, and when he ran backstage, Heather wrapped him up in a big robe. He seemed excited to meet both of them and was very personable, funny, and witty. Later, when Loretta would call their home to talk to Heather, Paul often answered. He'd talk about how they were potty training their daughter, Beatrice, and say how proud he was of Loretta and Heather and all they had overcome, proud of their positive attitudes and what they did to help others.

"He was really nice and extremely supportive," she told her mom the next day. "He's just a nice guy—someone you'd like to hang out with."

Loretta would have liked to wear her new hand to the concert, but it would be several more weeks before it was finished. Like everything else, she had a goal in mind, and she wanted to have her hand in time for Alyssa's *Nutcracker* performance. It had been nearly a year since the amputation, and she was ready to feel complete, to be totally reassembled. Alyssa had danced in *The Nutcracker* several times before, and every year Loretta always bought a new outfit to wear to the ballet. This year, she wanted to wear her new hand, too.

And yet, she was nervous to get it. She knew the finished product would be fabulous, but still, it was another reminder of what she didn't have, that she no longer had a hand and it had to be replaced.

That afternoon, the doorbell rang. It was Norm, and Loretta knew exactly what was in the UPS box. *If he only knew what he was delivering!* she thought. She took the package to the kitchen and set it on the table. For at least an hour, she just stared at it. Finally, she opened it up and … it looked exactly like her hand! It was just like looking at her own hand.

But she couldn't make herself put it on. She was afraid, but she didn't know why, so she just sat at the table and cried. The hand was so realistic. *But why do I even have to have a new hand?* Even though it was perfect, it was a symbol of the horror she'd been through. She knew she was being ridiculous. *I've been so upset about the ugly legs I have to wear, and now I have a hand that looks absolutely beautiful, and I'm upset about that, too.*

Loretta looked at the clock. The school bus was due, so she lifted the hand from the box and pulled it on like a glove. The fit was perfect.

She was still sitting at the kitchen table when her children came in. Her hands were folded under her chin. Alyssa took one look at her and cried, "Oh,

Mommy!" and ran in for a hug, thrilled to see her mom fully intact again.

A few hours later, Wally came home. He took the gold chain off her neck, held her left hand, and put her wedding rings back where they belonged.

PART THREE

Missing Parts

Although the world is full of suffering,
it is full also of the overcoming of it.

~Helen Keller

.

Chapter 17

If Loretta couldn't have the legs God gave her, she wanted the next best thing. Established in 1989, Dorset Orthopaedic opened under the direction of founder Bob Watts, prosthetist and managing director, and his wife, Tessa. The clinic is tucked in the picturesque Dorset County countryside, not far from Stonehenge in southwest England. Their mission is to produce the best possible artificial limbs and to be the top prosthetics center in the United Kingdom.

By the time Loretta met him, Bob had been in the prosthetics business for more than thirty years. Early on, he was the official prosthetist for the British Paralympic Team and had traveled with them to the 1992 Paralympics in Barcelona. As part of his duties, he tested each competitors' artificial limbs to the extreme and discovered that even the smallest adjustments to the alignment could improve the athlete's track time.

From this experience, Bob learned how to deliver the maximum function to each prosthetic, and he took that knowledge back to his own company. Through trial and error, he learned how to produce prosthetic limbs that felt realistic and also functioned the way he thought they should. He experimented with a high-quality silicone—a product that was already being used in Belgium to make natural looking arms, noses, and ears—to make attractive covers for his prosthetics, and his effort paid off. Dorset limbs are tailored and sculpted to match the body and to blend in with the patient's skin, and instead of producing heavy, clunky legs like Loretta had, they manufacture custom legs that are beautiful and lifelike.

In 1993, Bob read a news article about a young model named Heather Mills who had been hit by a police motorcycle in London. She stepped off a curb, was hit by the bike, and her left leg was severed below the knee. Bob thought he could help, so he reached out to her.

Heather had seen what prosthetic legs looked like, and she wasn't happy with her choices. She didn't understand why realistic-looking legs weren't available, especially when they routinely made lifelike figures at Madame Tussaud's wax museum.

"If they can make wax figures look so real," she asked him, "why can't there be prosthetic limbs that look that good? If people can buy designer clothes, why can't amputees purchase a beautiful leg?"

Using Heather as his guinea pig, Bob developed a new product, a silicone cosmetic cover that was applied over the artificial leg. It looked and felt real, and the result was a resounding success. The product not only allowed her to walk in comfort, but the combination of a well-built leg and a realistic-looking cover gave Heather back her life. Wearing a pretty leg helped her come to terms with the amputation, to regain her self-esteem, and to enjoy normal activities again.

"We made the leg," Bob said, "and Heather made it sexy."

Her leg was beautiful, but the most important feature was its comfortable socket. If the socket wasn't comfortable, it didn't really matter how beautiful the leg was because if it didn't feel right, she couldn't wear it. Heather now contends that she can do just about anything she did before her amputation— and can even do what many women who have both of their natural legs can't do. She is a competitive skier on the Paralympic team, has been a contestant on the TV show *Dancing With The Stars,* has competed on Britain's *Dancing on Ice*—and she even wears five-inch heels with a short skirt when she wants to.

Dorset's onsite factory has a number of technicians who take the patients' measurements, mold the limbs, and help their clients select a skin color. To the casual observer, it looks a lot like a mannequin factory. Arms and legs are propped on tables at all angles, and artists bend over them to paint the intricate details of the nails and the skin, adding freckles and hair where appropriate. They will even add a tattoo if the client requests it.

Loretta had her heart set on going to Dorset for new legs. She wanted her independence and self-confidence back, and since she'd always been something of a glamour girl, the promise of having attractive and fully functional legs boosted her spirits and, therefore, accelerated her recovery.

The standard practice at Dorset was to wait at least a year after an amputation before being fitted for the high-end prosthetics. Loretta's residual legs had to finish healing and shrink down to their final size, to ensure that she got the best possible fit for what would, hopefully, become her permanent legs. She and Wally made an appointment for the spring of 2003.

Before then, Loretta had never wanted to travel outside the U.S., particularly not after 9/11, but the prospect of getting new legs changed her mind. They climbed aboard a British Airways flight and took the red eye to London. Of course, she was still wearing the ugly bubble legs that gave her blisters and restricted how far she could walk.

To relieve the pressure on the flight, she popped the legs loose, but she was afraid to take off the liners because she didn't know if they could get them back on. She didn't sleep much on the overnight flight, and when they arrived, Loretta was tired. She had to ask for a wheelchair, which she didn't like to do, but she couldn't possibly have managed all the escalators and stairs in the airport while pulling her luggage. Thanks to the wheelchair, they were whisked through the airport. It was fun, but Loretta had never been to Heathrow Airport and had no idea it would be so crazy and chaotic. She was fascinated to see people of all nationalities going in every direction.

They'd made it to London, but they still had quite a journey ahead of them; it was a network of planes, trains, and automobiles. They had to change trains multiple times to get closer to New Forest, where they had booked a room in a bed and breakfast that wasn't far from Dorset Orthopaedic in nearby Ringwood. But the trains didn't go all the way to New Forest, so they reserved a rental car for the final leg of their trip. Some of their trains were delayed, and their travel took forever, and by the time they arrived to pick up the car, the agency had closed for the day.

By this time, Loretta was beyond exhausted. She'd been up all night, had been unable to budget her steps, and was overtaxed from stepping up and off train platforms, weaving in and out of crowds, and shuffling luggage. She'd walked too far for too long, and her clunky legs delivered their expected blisters.

She sat down on the curb and started to cry.

Then, to top it off, it started raining.

But as Loretta has often said, "Every time I was in real need, God put an angel in the right place at the right time." This particular angel came in the form of an Englishman named Ian who drove a little black sports car and took pity on the drenched American couple who were sitting on the side of the road. He pulled over and asked if he could help. Wally told him their sob story and, before they knew it, Ian had crammed all of their luggage into the tiny car, and off they went.

The owner of the B&B ultimately became a great friend, and the next morning, she let Wally drive her Land Rover to take Loretta to her appointment at Dorset. Later, she took Wally to get their rental car.

Driving in England was a whole new experience. The roads can be very narrow, and the British drive on the left side of the road, rather than the right. One time they were driving down one of the notorious English shrub lanes—paths that are so narrow in spots that you have to pull over to let the other car pass—and they clipped mirrors with the oncoming car. This would most likely have turned into an ordeal in the States, but the other driver acted like it was nothing and kept on going.

When they arrived at Dorset Orthopaedic, Loretta was a little surprised that a company headquartered in such a modest environment could produce such high-end artificial limbs. Yet, the unpretentious atmosphere is part of Dorset's charm, and Loretta liked the fact that the clinic was warm and friendly, rather than huge and sterile. She'd been in too many hospitals like that. Wally checked her in and then left to go get their rental car. It would take several hours to complete her initial consultation and measurements, and he knew he would be back well before they were finished.

Being fitted for a prosthesis at Dorset is a multi-step process. The limb is built incrementally, and there are numerous calculations and decisions to be made. A fitting cannot be accomplished in a single appointment, and Loretta had several sessions scheduled. On the first day, her prosthetist measured and wrapped her residual legs, then cast molds that would later be filled with plaster of Paris and used to make her prosthetics. Next, they calculated the precise length for her new legs, which, in her case, was a challenge. For single-leg amputees, it's a simple process of measuring the other leg and duplicating its length. But in Loretta's case, they had to calculate the length, and it was important to be accurate. She needed to have the right amount of leg extension to allow her to sit comfortably in a chair without causing her knees to be too high or too low.

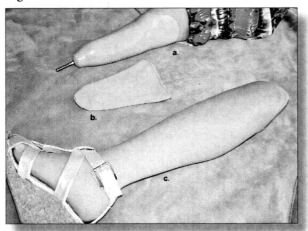

Liner with pin (a), sock (b), and socket with silicone cover (c)

Underneath the silicone covers, the legs are high-tech and well-engineered, and two important components are crafted that allow the limb to attach to the patient's natural leg: *the liner* and *the socket*. *The liner* is made from a tight silicone material that the patient wears over the residual limb. It has a pin on the end that locks into the socket with an audible snap. *The socket* is the concave area at the top of the prosthetic leg that accepts the pin from the liner. To put on the prosthetic, the patient pulls on the liner and a protective sock, then snaps the pin into the socket, much like plugging a phone into a car charger. To take the leg off, the patient presses an invisible button on the leg, usually marked by a freckle, to release—or pop off—the leg.

At Loretta's first fitting, Dorset had the mechanical parts of her legs put together, but hadn't yet created the cosmetic covers that would make them look like natural legs. "You could see all of the innards," she later told her mother. "They didn't look like real legs at all. I felt like I was in a sci-fi movie. There was a wall of mirrors where I could see my reflection, and my top half looked human, but down below, I could see these mechanical, robotic legs."

It was time to test them out. Loretta's prosthetist helped her put them on and asked her to walk around. He watched intently, observing her stride, and then called her over to tighten or loosen a screw here and there, to fine-tune the fit.

After that, they concentrated on her new feet and began the design of the silicone covers that would ultimately become intricate works of art. For single-leg amputees, a new foot is designed based on the patient's remaining foot, but since Loretta was a bilateral amputee, they asked her to bring in old photographs of her feet. But she'd never taken pictures of them, so she searched through dozens of magazines and catalogs, looking for pictures of feet that resembled her own, which she cut out and brought with her. She also brought along a pair of shoes with 2½-inch heels that they used to mold the contours of the prosthetic feet.

There were so many things to consider. They designed the width of the foot and ankle, the Achilles tendon, the details and variations of the skin, and the size and length of the toes. They even asked, "Should your second toe be longer than your big toe, or do you want the toes to decrease in size from the big toe on down?" Creating individual toes that are separate from one another is called "toe cleavage," a mark of quality in the industry and a desirable aspect in the design of lifelike limbs.

She had a break between appointments that lasted several days, so she and Wally decided to take a side trip. They took the bullet train under the English Channel and went to Paris for three days of sightseeing. "It was all very exciting," Loretta said. "And even though I felt a lot of joy about being in Paris, I cried at times, too. I was in the most romantic city in the world, but I was still wearing those ugly legs, and I was in perpetual pain from all the walking. I just wasn't in any shape to be touring."

After their quick excursion, they returned to the clinic, and when her fittings were complete, Wally and Loretta flew back home while her legs were being constructed. A month later, they went back to England to pick them up, and this time, Mitch and Alyssa went with them. Loretta was eager to introduce them to Heather.

Heather had done so much for Loretta, and she wanted to take her a gift— but what do you give Paul McCartney's wife? Saying "thank you" didn't seem to be enough, so she tried to think about how to express her true gratitude. Loretta's friend, Carolyn, designed jewelry, and she made Loretta a beaded bracelet that said *Faith, Hope, Love.* During some of her most difficult days, those words grounded and strengthened Loretta. The bracelet seemed like a perfect gift for Heather, so she asked Carolyn to make another one. When Loretta was at her wits' end, feeling more than sad and completely overwhelmed, that's exactly what Heather had given her—faith, hope, and love.

A welcoming committee was waiting in the parking lot at Dorset when they arrived—Bob Watts, Heather, and her film crew, who were there to capture the visit for future use in Heather's philanthropic work. Mitch and Alyssa asked Heather to autograph the ad they'd brought with them, the one that initially caught Wally's attention and alerted him that glamour legs even existed. She was happy to do so.

They made their way inside, and the excited chatter of the meet-and-greet died down to a nervous anticipation. The Goebels had been through this before. The whole family knew what it was like to be all torqued up, only to crash and burn with disappointment. This time they were more reserved, and they dialed back their emotions.

The cameras were rolling. Loretta sat down, and her prosthetist pulled on the liners. He popped on her new legs, and Loretta grinned. "They're beautiful! They look so real. And I even have toe cleavage!" she giggled.

It was a good start, but the moment of truth was still ahead. Loretta stood up and was very cautious. "They feel pretty good," she said, then took a few steps. A dazzling smile lit up her face. "I think I could get used to these real easy," she said. "They feel good. I *love* them!"

She smiled at the kids, and relief spread over them like a warm summer sunrise. They watched her walk with obvious comfort, looking like Mom again in her 2-½ inch heels and perfect toes—tall, blonde, and beautiful.

Loretta was back.

When they had a private moment, Loretta gave Heather the bracelet. "I've been trying to find a way to thank you for everything you've done for me," she said, tears welling in her eyes, "so I had this made for you." She offered the bracelet to Heather. "See, it matches mine," she said and showed Heather her own. "It was made with love and given with love, and I wanted you to have one, too."

Heather was touched. She hugged Loretta and gave her a kiss on the cheeks, and she put the bracelet on. Loretta knew that Heather had a lot of incredible jewelry and hoped that even if she never wore the bracelet and tossed it in the bottom of a drawer, that whenever she came across it, she would remember Loretta and know how much she'd meant to her recovery.

Heather invited them to come to her home in London, and when they arrived the next day, Loretta was pleased to see that she was still wearing the bracelet. Heather and Paul's home was neat and tidy. The rooms had very high ceilings, but the house was not large considering who they were, although it was quite elaborate. They got comfortable in the great room, and Maria, the housekeeper, served them snacks—little short cans of Coke that weren't available in the States yet and some "crisps" that Americans call potato chips.

Mitch and Alyssa went outside to play with their dog, Oliver, and they had fun roughhousing with him. Loretta looked to the other side of the room. An old piano drew her attention and she walked over to it. "What's this?" she asked Heather.

"That's Paul's original upright. He's kept it all these years," she answered. "Look on the wall above it."

Loretta leaned in and looked at what she had thought might be a picture, but it wasn't. It was the original score of "Yesterday," magnificently framed and on display. Once again, she was struck by the bizarre path that had led her to this room. *Who would have ever thought that a girl from Shipman, Illinois, would be in the home of Sir Paul McCartney?*

They stayed for a couple of hours and then had to get on the road. They were driving back to the B&B that evening because Loretta had some final leg appointments the next morning. Just a few days later, they flew back home.

In July 2003, shortly after Loretta received the final version of her glamour legs, Bob and Tessa Watts of Dorset Orthopaedic, traveled to Boston for a conference sponsored by the Amputee Coalition of America. Loretta served as the model in Dorset's tradeshow booth, and Heather was the guest speaker at the conference. Other experts in the industry stopped by the Dorset booth, and Bob always challenged them to guess which of the four of them—Bob, Tessa, Loretta, or Wally—was the amputee. Not a single person guessed that it was Loretta. She was, as usual, busy moving about here and there and chatting it up with everyone, wearing sandals that showed off her perfectly painted toenails and her new toe ring. Since Wally was the one sitting in a chair at the back of the booth, everyone figured that he was the amputee.

Bob loved that climactic moment when he revealed that Loretta was his patient. "Now guess which one of her legs is the prosthesis," he challenged, but they couldn't figure that out either. No one ever guessed that Loretta had two artificial legs.

That fall, Loretta and Wally went back to Dorset to have her legs adjusted. They visited Heather in London again, and she was very "prettily pregnant," according to Loretta. At the time, the McCartneys were interviewing for a nanny, and they all joked that Loretta's picture would probably land on the front page of the paper the next day because she'd gotten out of the car to push the button that opened the huge gate at the end of their driveway. They wondered if the headlines would identify her as the McCartneys' new nanny.

"I have to offer a bit of an apology," Heather said. "I thought we could all have dinner together, but Paul is running late and is still at the studio."

Of course, they would have enjoyed having dinner with both Heather and Paul, but being with Heather was the most important thing to Loretta. She had always admired Paul McCartney—and who wouldn't—but Heather was the one who took her hand, showed her the way, and ushered her out of that deep, dark tunnel. Heather was Loretta's hero.

They spent a lot of time in her kitchen that day, and Heather made herself a decaf soy latte and other snacks that fit her vegetarian lifestyle. They talked about losing their limbs, and Heather asked Loretta if she had experienced the phantom pain that often haunts amputees. "I still feel it myself, even after all these years," she said.

"I haven't had to deal with that," Loretta answered. "Maybe it's because my limbs died slowly and were then removed, and my brain adjusted along the way. It's probably completely different when a leg is suddenly severed. I can't imagine dealing with false pain on top of the agony of my first legs."

"Will you do me a favor?" Heather asked. "Now that you're not using them, would you mind shipping me those legs?"

Heather wanted to use the legs as a visual aid when she was interviewed on various television programs. She wanted to contrast those plastic, clunky legs to her own slender one. True to her word, when she was a guest on *Larry King Live* later that month, she talked about the various problems involved with acquiring comfortable and nice-looking prosthetics, and then she showed Larry and the audience Loretta's original legs.

"It isn't vain to want to wear something that looks real like this," Heather said, pointing to her own leg. "You don't like looking at your leg and having that reminder every day that you can't wear your skirt, that you can't feel feminine, that you can't feel normal because everyone is looking at you every two minutes. And on top of that, her socket was so uncomfortable that she couldn't walk with the huge legs," she told Larry. Then she showed a clip of Loretta talking with Heather backstage at Paul's concert. She clearly needed something different.

Loretta was delighted to be a part of Heather's work, and she actually felt that their roles were mutually beneficial. Heather was a crusader who urged amputees to seek out the best prostheses that were available. But everyone knew that she could afford whatever she wanted, which could potentially undermine her message. In contrast, Loretta was a common person, like most amputees, and when Heather told Loretta's story, it was proof that attractive prostheses were accessible to everyone, not just the rich and famous. And since Heather operated in an international arena, Loretta's reach was extended, and she was able to touch far more lives than she ever could on her own.

"That's why I think God placed Loretta from Shipman with Paul McCartney's wife," she said, "because we could help each other in different ways."

Heather was inextricably linked with Dorset and with Bob and Tessa Watts, who wanted to reach out to amputees everywhere—especially those who suffered the most, but had the least. Loretta admired that, and she enjoyed hearing Bob and Heather tell stories about their trips to Croatia, when they took truckloads of limbs to people who had lost their own to land mines.

"The more people we can help, the better," Tessa affirmed.

Loretta and Wally not only became close friends with Bob and Tessa, but with the rest of the staff at Dorset. Throughout her numerous appointments, the technicians and prosthetists helped Loretta realize that amputations weren't all that uncommon, and that they happened to all kinds of people, everywhere. They stressed the importance for all amputees to find the right help, draw on their inner strength, and get on with life—and to be responsible for their own futures.

It was Dorset's job to provide a comfortable leg, but Loretta still has to strike a delicate balance to sustain that comfort. She must maintain a consistent body weight, so her legs continue to fit properly. If she gains a few pounds, the legs get tight and pinch and can even cut off her circulation, which makes her hips go numb. On the other hand, the legs get loose and shift around if she loses weight, which not only makes it hard for her to walk because she feels unstable, but loose legs can cause blisters.

For the first few years, Loretta's residual legs continued to atrophy and change shape, and she went back to Dorset several times to have the sockets refitted. After six years, her limbs finally stabilized, and refitting was not needed as often. She does, however, get occasional cosmetic fixes when her legs develop what she calls "silicone stretch marks," and Dorset repairs them by pulling the silicone back up and tightening it—sort of like a facelift below the knees.

She eventually got a sportier pair of legs that she wears when she rides her bike or exercises, which she calls her "tennis shoe legs."

"My tennis shoe legs are for exercise or when I'm traipsing around outside, and I usually wear them around the house, too. Glamour legs are made for high heels, and that's what I normally wear in public. In fact, I wear them about 95 percent of the time. But when you get home, you want to kick those heels off. That's when I switch to my tennis shoe legs, which are my slippers, so to speak."

Her exercise legs have flat feet and what is called a College Park Ankle. The ankles on her glamour legs move in only two directions, frontward and backward, but the College Park Ankle moves in all four directions like a natural ankle does—frontward, backward, and side to side, making it much more amenable to exercise.

Wally had bought Loretta a three-wheeled bike, and as soon as she got the new legs, she wanted to ride it. Sycamore was in a rural community, and one day she rode out north on a country road where she'd be far from any traffic. It was a beautiful fall day, and a strong sun bathed the earth. She rode past a field and saw a farmer harvesting corn on his combine. The machine churned the corn and kicked up all kinds of dust clouds, but it also set swarms of bugs flying.

Loretta hadn't expected that. The bugs flew into her face and swarmed around her head, and she swatted at them in defense. Preoccupied with the bugs, she didn't realize she'd almost reached the corner. She wasn't turning the bike sharply enough, so she gave the handlebars a hard shove with her left hand—the artificial one—and made it around the turn. But she was so sweaty that her hand flew off her arm and fell into the ditch.

"I could just picture that farmer going home at noon to a nice lunch all set out on the table and telling his wife, *I just saw the darndest thing out there while combining. This girl on a bike flung her hand clean into the ditch!*"

Loretta got off her bike, walked over to the ditch, and picked up her hand. "And how can you not laugh? I was more worried about the farmer who had just witnessed that scene than about being embarrassed about flinging my hand off. It was so funny!"

Loretta really liked her exercise legs and the ankles, in particular, so she asked the technicians if they could put a College Park Ankle on a heeled leg. "We've never tried it before, especially not on a bilateral amputee," they said, "but we'll give it a shot." So they made her a second set of glamour legs with ankles that had a full range of motion.

Right away, she noticed some differences. The new ankles were thicker than on her other legs, and she didn't feel as confident in her stride because they tended to wobble a little. But they were better if she was walking downhill toward the street or standing side-to-side on a slope. Although she uses both sets, she wears her original design most of the time.

"But if I'm wearing a brown outfit, and there's a brown pair of shoes on one pair of legs, those are the ones I wear. And if I want to wear black shoes, I'll switch to the legs with the black shoes. And sometimes I switch back and forth because the legs can wear on me, like shoes do. If you're getting a blister from a pair of shoes, you switch to a different pair, right? That's what I do with my legs. And both sets were designed so I can wear shoes with 2½-inch heels—and I have a lot of them."

So much for the guy who told her she'd never wear heels again.

Chapter 18

Though she was thrilled with her new legs, Loretta had a long journey ahead to recover what she missed the most—her independence. She was still at the mercy of everyone else because she couldn't do the most basic things for herself. At first, Alyssa had to learn how to help her get dressed, and they made it a game they called "Dress the Mommy." Alyssa would pull a top over her mother's head, zip up her pants, button her sweater, and help her put on her legs.

"Alyssa literally had to help me put on whatever I wanted to wear, or she helped me with my jewelry, and she was only seven years old! I should have been 'bunning' her hair for dance lessons and instead, my little girl is putting on the backs of my earrings or helping me put my liners on, just so I could wear my legs."

The liners were a major obstacle for Loretta because she couldn't get them on or off by herself. Made from extremely tight silicone that fits over the residual leg, to take a liner off, she started at the top and rolled it down her leg. To put it back on, she had to position it just right on her natural leg and pull it back up, something she could have easily done if she had two hands, but her right thumb and partial forefinger were not strong enough to pull up the tight silicone by themselves.

To control how her legs fit from one day to the next, she wore a sock over the liner. If she lost weight, she put on a thicker sock to tighten things up, because if the legs were too loose, it was like walking around in old Army boots, or in shoes that were too big. It affected her balance and she felt totally insecure in her stride. If she gained weight, she wore a thinner sock because if the legs were too tight, they cut off her circulation and made her bottom go numb. She called it doing "sock math," which was the trial-and-error method of getting the thickness just right.

More than anything, Loretta wanted to do it by herself, but if Wally wasn't home, Mitch or Alyssa had to help her. There were so many times when she would be home alone, wanting to do this, that, and the other thing, but she couldn't. She wanted to ride the exercise bike while the kids were at school, and afterward she would need to take a bath, which meant she'd have to take her legs and liners off. But she couldn't get them back on by herself and would need to pick Alyssa up after school or stop at the grocery store to get something for dinner. So she always had to coordinate her schedule around someone being home to put her legs back on.

This went on for *four* years.

"I couldn't stand it," Loretta said. "I had to figure it out. So when I finally had enough strength to hold the liner tight enough between my thumb and finger to pull it up my leg, that was significant. I was like, *Oh my goodness, I can put my legs on by myself, and I am not going back!"*

There was nothing good about being dependent on Alyssa, and Loretta often grieved about their ridiculous role-reversal. *I should be taking care of my children, not making them take care of me.* Initially, Alyssa didn't mind helping her mom, but when she turned ten, things changed. They flew to Scottsdale to meet Mary Phelan and her daughter, Kelli, where they stayed at a resort. Of course, Alyssa wanted to run off and do things with Kelli instead of being stuck taking care of her mom, and Loretta certainly couldn't blame her. But she still needed Alyssa's help.

"My legs were terrible then. The flight had really messed me up, and I had retained water, so my legs were really thick. I couldn't get the sock ply right, and we had to constantly re-do the liners. I was in terrible pain that whole weekend."

Mary was one of Loretta's best friends, but given their glamour mom history, it was hard for Loretta to let Mary see how needy she was. It was one thing to say, "Can you fix this necklace?" or "Can I borrow your mascara?" But it was completely different to ask for help with something that she physically could not do for herself. She simply couldn't show that weakness to Mary; it was just too humbling. So Alyssa was on the hook.

"We stayed in a room with two queen beds, and even though we'd planned to sleep with our own daughters, Mary and I ended up sharing one bed and the girls took the other one. That first night, we finished dinner and everyone had taken their bath, and here I came, walking out of the bathroom on my knees. It was *so* hard to show myself to Mary that way. And she knew everything that had happened to me! She'd been through it with me, but still, I couldn't stand for her to see me all whittled away."

And for the first time, Alyssa didn't want to help.

Loretta's leg had blistered because her liners were too tight, and when they were out by the pool she said, "Alyssa, I'm uncomfortable, can you please help me re-do my leg?"

Alyssa balked. "Mom, Kelli wants me to go to the water slide."

With no one to help her, Loretta sat by the pool and cried—out of frustration, out of pain, out of embarrassment—out of complete helplessness.

The night before they went home, they had planned a nice dinner as their last hurrah, but Loretta couldn't even eat. Her pain was so intense that she could feel her pulse beating in her shin bones.

"Alyssa, can we please go in the bathroom?" she asked. She needed to pull off her liners and reposition them.

Alyssa huffed and puffed. She rolled her eyes and scowled at her mother. "Again?" she asked.

Loretta stood up and walked to the bathroom, an annoyed Alyssa trailing behind her. She closed the door and burst into tears. "Do you think I like asking my ten-year-old to help me? No, I don't. Please, just help me one more time!"

Loretta yearned for her life to go back to the way it had been before. She wanted to be able to do what she'd always done with her kids, like spend time in the yard, run here, run there, it didn't really matter what; she just wanted to do something active and fun. And she didn't want Mitch and Alyssa to have to worry about helping her. It seemed so backward to ask her children to take care of her, but without their help, she was lost.

One night, Wally was mowing the lawn, and Loretta wanted to go outside and do something fun with Mitch, but she had a big knot on the back of her knee, a blistered welt where the liner had pinched. She walked into the family room and apologized to him.

"I'm sorry, Mitch. The weather is beautiful, and we should be outside doing something fun, but I just can't."

She popped off her leg, and when Mitch saw the welt, he started to cry.

"It's okay Mom," he sniffed. "You didn't ask for any of this." Then he went to the kitchen and brought her an ice pack, staying inside the rest of the evening with his mother.

Taking care of their home had always been important to Loretta, but now nothing came easy. She had to re-learn how to do everything. The simple, everyday tasks that she used to take for granted, like setting the table with her own plates and glasses, now seemed impossible. Her dishes were made of pottery, so they were thick and heavy, and to get a plate from the kitchen cabinet to the table was a nightmare. She had to grab it with her thumb and partial forefinger to pick it up, but she didn't have the strength to carry them all the way to the table. Without fingers, the everyday things in life seemed insurmountable.

"And just try to make your kids a sandwich! Without a left hand, I couldn't hold the piece of bread still. I'd try to smear something on it— and it would move. I was literally chasing it across the counter. I'd put the peanut butter jar under my left arm to try to unscrew the lid, and once I accomplished that, I was chasing the bread and fighting to keep control of it while smearing on the peanut butter. It was not fun."

She also struggled to do laundry. Her washer had a knob that she had to pull out to get it started, but without fingers, she couldn't get behind the knob to pull it. She remembered that when she'd first gone to rehab, her therapist had given her a thin, blue cloth for gripping. She dug the cloth out of the drawer and draped it over the knob, pulled it out, and started the washer by herself.

Her therapist also encouraged her to learn to drive again and suggested that she take a driving class in downtown Chicago, but Loretta would have none of that. She would never have driven in Chicago on a good day with both her legs, and she was certainly not going to do it now. There wasn't much traffic near where they lived, so that seemed like a much better option. When they got back to Sycamore, she told Wally, "Get in—because I am figuring this out."

Wally got in and started the car from the passenger side, and Loretta gave it a shot. She familiarized herself with the pedals and how to apply the appropriate pressure to accelerate, and then she wanted to practice braking. Like a new driver, she hit the brake, and they both flew forward. She hit the brake again, and they bucked forward again, a scene that repeated itself several times until she got it mastered. Now she's so experienced that there's no problem, but that first day, it was a rough ride. All that time, Wally wasn't wearing his seat belt.

"What are you doing? Why don't you have your seat belt on?" she asked him.

"Are you kidding?" he said. "If I need to get out, I'm getting out fast!"

Loretta threw her head back and laughed. "Well, thanks for the vote of confidence, Wally!"

After hours of practice, Loretta learned to drive again, but she still didn't have the independence she craved because she couldn't turn the key far enough to spark the ignition. Handling the key could also be a problem. She had to pinch it with the teeth pointed in the right direction, but if she didn't pinch it tight enough, she dropped it. If her grip was good, she put the key in just deep enough so that it wouldn't fall out, then pushed it in the rest of the way with the heel of her hand. But even with all that effort, she still couldn't turn the key far enough to start the car.

"When you're used to hauling yourself and everyone else here and there and yonder, and you want to run out to get coffee, or you want to run to the store because the new Michael Buble Christmas CD is out—you want to do that on your own! I never wanted to ask for help because that made me a burden. I couldn't stand it that someone else had to schedule their day around hauling me into town. But I couldn't turn on the car, which meant I could never go anywhere by myself. And I tried and tried to start the car, but I could never do it."

In the summer of 2002, the year before she got her glamour legs, Wally's sister, Nancy, came to help Loretta. "I was there for moral support," Nancy said. "Loretta was determined. She wanted to do her own dishes, ironing, and grocery shopping, and we tried to figure out a way for her to do it all by herself."

Every day Nancy wanted Loretta to try something new. Like a gentle drill sergeant, she pushed Loretta to try all sorts of things. She'd say, "Let's try this," or "Let's do that now," or "Let's figure this out."

One day Nancy said, "Come on Loretta, let's see if you can start the car."

It was Nancy's idea to use the blue gripper cloth. She thought it might give Loretta the traction she needed to turn the key. Loretta went out to the garage with Nancy and the kids, got in the car, and put the key halfway in. She pushed it in further with the heel of her hand and draped the blue gripper around it, then reached her wrist waaaaay down under, turned the key, and *BAM!* It started the first time.

Mitch and Alyssa screamed, and they jumped up and down like she'd just won the lottery.

Loretta laughed out loud, looked at her fans and said, "Alright! Everyone in for Target!" They took off like a group of teenagers heading off for spring break.

"It was thrilling when Loretta learned to turn the car key," Nancy said, "because it was so important to her. Given time, the muscles in her right hand became more flexible, and she was able to turn the key without the blue gripper, once she figured out how to place it just right and apply the correct amount of pressure."

That same week, Loretta started driving by herself. Mitch was in summer track, and she drove him to practice. She waited in the car for him and cried the whole time, so grateful that she could do a simple thing like take her son to practice. In the past she would have thought, *I have to take Mitch to track, and it's so dang hot out,* but now she sat in the car and thought, *Thank you, God, that I am still alive and am able to do this and be here for my son.* Loretta was starting to see everything in her life with new eyes.

Driving alone was a major milestone, but Loretta continued to have setbacks over smaller tasks. She was home alone one day and wanted some chips and salsa, but the salsa was in the bottom corner of the pantry. She couldn't get down on her knees with her prosthetics on to fish it out, so she tried to use the broom to sweep it out. But the salsa was way back in the corner under a shelf, and the broom wouldn't angle enough to reach it. And even if she did get it out, she couldn't unscrew the top—not to mention that she couldn't open a bag of chips. That broke Nancy's heart, so she reorganized Loretta's pantry and bought her a jar opener called 'Lids Off.' Now there was one more thing she could do by herself.

Loretta continued to push on. At first she didn't grocery shop alone because she couldn't get things off the shelf if it had been freshly stocked and the products were too close together. She couldn't get in and around an item to grasp it. And if something was in a plastic container, it wouldn't be a big deal if she dropped it, but if she wanted to get dill pickles or jelly, or spaghetti sauce in a glass jar, she couldn't risk that. Over time, she developed more strength and devised her own way of doing things, and she can handle almost anything now. "In fact, I can wrap a mean Christmas present! You'd think it had been wrapped at Macy's."

While Nancy was visiting, she helped Loretta get back on track in many ways, but eventually, she had to return to Michigan. "I never had children of my own, and I always wondered why," Nancy said. "I think God knew I'd need to be available to help Loretta and Wally." Not only was she there to help that summer, but over the next couple of years, she made many trips to Sycamore to stay with the children when Loretta and Wally went back to England, and she helped them in countless other ways. She was fortunate to have an understanding boss who told her to put her family first and let her have a flexible schedule.

The first summer, Loretta worked hard to jump back into her prior life as much as she could. She popped on her painful "bubble legs" and adjusted her wig, then went out and taught Vacation Bible School like she always had, and she also arranged the music program at church. She was not going to let life pass her by, no matter what. As often as she could, she packed up the kids and drove the four hours to Shipman to see her family. She joked that if she ever got stopped for speeding she would say, "I'm sorry officer, but I have a lead foot." If he didn't believe her, she'd simply pop one off and show him.

Christmas of 2002 marked the one-year anniversary of her illness, and as a special treat for Loretta, Wally's mother invited almost fifty of their friends and family members to Michigan for the holiday. "Wally's mom asked us to come for Christmas and said that if I would give her my recipes, she would fix everything I had intended to cook the year I was sick. Everything that I had planned, everything I would have served them the year before, she was now going to make and serve to our family and friends. She incorporated every detail, even down to the candles and napkins. It was awesome. I loved it. She gave me back the Christmas that I lost."

Soon after the holidays, Loretta felt inspired to speak to her congregation at church. She was convinced that her church family had played a significant role in her recovery. "I believe in miracles, and I believe in the power of prayer," she told them. "It is by the power of answered prayer that I stand here today. Thank you for all your support."

And yet, even after a year, she still could not fully comprehend what had happened to her. She wrote in her journal: *This morning, I woke up after a good night's sleep to the sun on my face. I felt great and well rested, ready to confront the day, and all seemed fine until I got ready to get up, and reality hit once again that I have no legs to get out of bed! For a brief moment all seemed normal and then … it's not.*

The shock she had experienced took a long time to subside, and another year later she wrote: *I don't even recognize myself. The old me had long straight hair, long fingers, and muscular calves. I didn't have scars on my side and mouth. I didn't complain and my pace was much faster. I enjoyed walking for exercise, which I haven't been able to do, and I enjoyed cooking, which is now a chore because of the pain in my legs. I miss me!*

And she constantly worried about how she was causing others to suffer. She thought about her mother and how she must be hurting. "As a mother, I can't imagine what it would be like to watch my child go through a life-threatening illness, only to end up losing their limbs," she said. "I feel sad about how my mom must grieve for me when there's nothing she can do about it."

Loretta was right. There was nothing anyone could do.

Chapter 19

Wally and Loretta started talking about selling their home and moving to a house that had a first-floor master bedroom, which they thought might be better for Loretta. Their bedroom was on the second floor, and Loretta wasn't sure if she wanted to continue to climb the stairs.

"If we're going to build again," Wally said, "we may as well move downstate to be near your parents and sisters." He felt certain he could transfer to Lambert International Airport in St. Louis, which was just across the river from Illinois and near the general area where Loretta's family lived. Even so, it was hard for Loretta to think about leaving her home and the people in Sycamore.

It was the only home their children had known, and Loretta had poured her life into making it a sanctuary for her family. "You could walk around our house in Sycamore, and everything in it had a story to tell, or had a specific person that was connected to it, someone who had helped us make it what it was. It was hard for me to think about giving it up."

But Loretta didn't have a choice. Wally made the decision to sell the house. They had talked about moving in general terms, but hadn't agreed to any specific plans. The discussions were always framed in "What if we …" or "Maybe we should …" but they never sat down and made a plan like they had always done before. As far as Loretta was concerned, moving was an idea to consider, but she hadn't quite warmed up to it yet.

One afternoon she looked out the back window and saw a "For Sale by Owner" sign tacked to a tree in their backyard. It hadn't been there that morning. Loretta caught her breath. *What was this?* Wally didn't tell her they were selling the house. *Why would he do that?* she wondered. Wally never made major decisions without consulting her, and she felt sick, betrayed. *Why didn't he talk to me first?*

Their house sat on an acre of woods, and another neighborhood backed up to their lot. The back yards were somewhat connected, but the For Sale sign could only be seen from one particular angle. *No one can even see the sign unless they're driving around the cul-de-sac behind us,* she thought, *but so what? Wally shouldn't have done this. We're supposed to be partners, but now it's like I hit my hand and lost control of my entire life.* Loretta was in turmoil, but she kept her feelings to herself. Wally probably had her best interests in mind.

The house sold within a week.

"If that's not an indication that we should sell the place, I don't know what would be," Wally said. "What are the chances that someone would drive around that circle, see the sign, and make an immediate offer?"

Her home wasn't the only thing she had trouble leaving behind. Loretta felt like she was being ripped from her community. Everywhere she went, people knew her, and she knew them. Before they moved away, she took the kids all over town and took pictures of the people who'd been important in their lives—their favorite girls at the deli at County Market, people at the grocery store, and Norm, the UPS man. They took all kinds of pictures of the places they loved and of their friends, the people who loved her and had prayed that she would live, and then held her hand and helped her through her illness and the amputations. Loretta and her family would be missed.

The Goebels moved in January 2004, and settled in Edwardsville, Illinois, about twenty-six miles across the river from St. Louis. They chose Edwardsville because it had an excellent school district and offered the kinds of activities their kids enjoyed. They decided to rent while they were building, and the house was about thirty minutes in each direction from Loretta's parents and all her sisters.

Adapting to the move was an effort, and Loretta was still upset about Wally selling the house. It was clear that he no longer considered her an equal in the relationship, that it wasn't a partnership anymore. *If he knew I was going to be like this, I don't think he would have married me. Why would he want to go through the hardship?*

But if she wanted to be happy, Loretta knew she had to stay positive. She went back to her tried and true formula for recovery and adaptation—faith, family, and friends—a combination that had always worked for her, before and after her illness. If she clung to those three things, she felt sure it would all work out fine.

But there were hurdles to cross. The people in Sycamore had been by her side through every stage of her illness and recovery, so she was not only accepted and embraced there, but the whole community went out of their way to help her, even anticipating her needs before she knew she had them. Now she was entering a world that didn't know her, knew nothing about her illness, her close brush with death, or her serial amputations. She meant nothing to the people in this community. It was intimidating, and it was scary.

"I was a stranger, and I was coming in as the 'new me,' the amputee, but I still wanted to be the glamour mom," Loretta said. "I didn't want to be labeled as handicapped. My motto was 'If you didn't know my story, you wouldn't know my loss.' By that, I meant that if you'd heard nothing about me and had just met me, you would never know that I had lost my legs and a hand."

Loretta concealed her amputations as best she could, which took a lot of energy because her legs might be killing her, but she swore she wouldn't walk with a limp. There were innumerable times when she was in the grocery store and was in pain, but she didn't want anyone to know about her situation, so her legs would just have to hurt until she got home. Early on, she scoped out every spot around town and in all the stores that had a place to sit down because she often had to stop and take a break.

Loretta always wore her prosthetic hand in public, but she never tried to hide the fact that she'd lost the fingers on her right hand. She actually had individual prosthetic fingers she could wear, but they were too cumbersome to make them worthwhile. Naturally, people noticed that her fingers were missing, particularly when she was at a checkout counter.

"The deli girl was one of the first to hear my story. As much as I didn't want anyone to know that I was an amputee, I did talk about it when people asked. It always started with questions about my missing fingers. And I'd say, 'Oh my goodness, if you only knew the whole story ...' and they'd say, 'Well, tell me!' So I'd tell them what happened, and inevitably I'd end up getting a hug. Then I'd hear comments like, 'I'll never feel sorry for myself again.' After that, they always sought me out every time I was in the store, just to visit. I loved that."

Loretta was quick to make friends, and because she never drew attention to herself in terms of her disabilities, her new community saw her as a victor, not a victim. They witnessed her strength and couldn't help but admire it. "And now, I'm not afraid to show my vulnerability. I can say, 'Okay, I have this pain going on' or 'I really need that case of soda, but I can't get it to my car.' I ask for help when I need it."

Since she didn't advertise her limitations, some people who had known Loretta for a long time didn't know she was an amputee. If they didn't ask questions, she didn't volunteer the information. In fact, she had lived in Edwardsville for several years when one of the other moms at Alyssa's dance studio finally heard about her history. She was flabbergasted.

"You mean you've lived here this long, and I never knew those weren't your legs?" she said. "I thought you must be a foot model because your feet are so perfect!"

Loretta laughed. "Well they should be—they're store bought. I'm not going to pay for corns and bunions—I want them to be perfect!"

Early on, the move was hard on the whole family, and it took some time for the kids to adjust. At first, Mitch had a hard time making friends. He was in sixth grade and, of course, middle school can feel like being thrown into the lion's den. The Goebels had moved in January, right in the middle of the school year, and by that time, it seemed like everyone else was part of a group.

"I don't like being new," Mitch told his mom. "Everyone already has friends, and I get left out."

Loretta nodded. "I'm in the same boat," she said. "You go to school every day, and you have to make new friends. I go to the bank, to the dry cleaners, the grocery store, the post office, to church, and I have to find a hair salon— all those things. I'm starting over, too." Mitch hadn't thought about the move being a struggle for his mother, and it helped to know he wasn't alone. It took a few months for him to figure things out, but he finally got settled.

Though Loretta was quick to make friends in the community, things weren't so comfortable at home. A rift had opened up between her and Wally, and the spark that had fueled them started to fizzle. Throughout their marriage, they always had clean lines that divided Loretta's responsibilities from Wally's. They were a tight team, yet very independent. They knew their own parts and where they intersected, and they each fulfilled their roles. But all that had changed and, out of necessity, Wally had taken over everything: his part, her part, and what they shouldered together. It should have been a temporary arrangement.

"Wally knew me, and I thought he should have known to turn my part back over to me, but he didn't. And even though I wanted my responsibilities back, I thought I should keep quiet because I felt indebted to him for putting up with me and all my problems. I knew I could never repay him. When something bothered me, I'd say to myself *This isn't that big of a deal* or *I can overlook that* until there were dozens of things that were no big deal, but they were festering under the surface, until everything felt like a huge, big deal. And I didn't know how to tell him to let me back in. I thought he should just know."

It was a new dynamic. Loretta and Wally weren't always on the same page anymore, even though their main priority was still the kids and helping them adapt to their new surroundings. Their relationship was suffering, but Loretta thought that with everything they'd been through—and now the move—that they were probably just going through an adjustment period, so she threw herself into what she'd always done, which was to make their home a haven.

They had gotten a good price for their house in Sycamore, had given up on the idea of a vacation home, and had settled most of their medical bills, so Loretta and Wally felt free to build a new house that would suit their needs for years to come. They worked with an architect to draw up the plans, but it was a messy process. Loretta wanted a nice home that would be wheelchair accessible to accommodate her potential future needs, but Wally wanted to make it a showplace, something that was much more elaborate than she thought they needed. The architect drew up several sets of plans, but invariably, Wally would think of something else, and they were back to the drawing board.

It didn't seem to matter that Loretta wanted something different. At first, she was on board with the plans. She wanted more space for their family and friends, but eventually she became disenchanted as it grew into what she viewed as a monstrosity.

Laura could tell that Loretta was upset, and it often made her sad for her sister, but she had no idea it had anything to do with Wally. "Why do you feel like you have to keep up the perfect you?" Laura asked. "Just relax and let yourself adapt. Let other people do things for you for a while. Don't worry so much about everything being perfect for now."

Distraught about her deteriorating relationship with Wally, Loretta did what she always did when faced with conflict: she retreated. In the past, she would have joined her family at night to watch TV, but now she lost herself in books. Practically all she did was read, sometimes devouring up to four books a week. Her method of coping was to climb in bed, snuggle under the covers by herself, and read.

But Loretta and the kids did enjoy going to Raging Rivers Water Park, and that summer she bought season passes. She put on her bikini again, even though the telltale scars on her right side were still somewhat visible. She liked to lounge by the pool, wearing cover-up pants that looked like something from *I Dream of Jeannie* and espradille sandals that laced up her legs. She didn't get in the water, but she loved to tan, and one day a man and his daughter stopped by her chair.

"I don't mean to bother you," the man said, "but my daughter is worried about you laying out in the sun with your shoes on. She's afraid the straps will leave tan marks all the way up your legs."

"Thanks for asking," Loretta answered "but my legs don't tan."

The man looked puzzled. "What do you mean?" he asked. She spent the next few minutes telling them her story, and it was one of those moments when she felt connected, and her heart was touched by how touched they were.

Children are usually quite adaptable, and Mitch and Alyssa were no exception. Once the initial shock of their mother's amputations wore off and they moved to Edwardsville, she was back to doing what she had always done, and life seemed normal to them, although it was a new normal.

"I usually take my left hand off when I'm at home," Loretta explained, "because it's so much easier for me to work around the house without it. To my family and friends, that's nothing out of the ordinary." But it could be quite a shock to the kids' friends, so before anyone new came to their house, Mitch and Alyssa would always say, "Don't freak out if my mom's hand is on the counter by the phone." That warning, coupled with Loretta's casual attitude, usually put their friends at ease, which is exactly what Loretta wanted to do.

Right away, she would joke with their friends about her amputations or say something to lighten the mood, so they wouldn't feel uncomfortable. She knew that most kids would be afraid to talk about such a thing, and she was concerned that they might even try to avoid her, but if she brought the subject up first, they were fine.

One day, Alyssa invited a group of friends over for a swim party. They came through the house and greeted Loretta, and Alyssa took them out back to the pool. A little while later, Loretta went outside to join them.

"Alyssa, do your friends know your mother comes in parts?" she said with a laugh. She sat down in the lawn chair and pulled off her arm, then stuffed it in her beach bag. Then she took off both her legs and leaned them against the chair, covering them with a towel to shield them from the hot sun. By now, everyone was watching. Loretta scooted out of the chair onto her knees, went to the side of the pool, and lowered herself into the water.

Most of the kids knew the basics of what had happened to her, but those who hadn't been around her very much were surprised—and intrigued—that Loretta wasn't embarrassed about being seen without her limbs. She certainly didn't seem self-conscious, which was impressive to teens who often were.

"That's really cool," one of the girls told Alyssa. "I think your mom is awesome."

To Loretta's delight, her children flourished in their new community, but she and Wally were losing ground, and the new house was their pressure point. Where they once agreed on almost everything, they now had different goals. Everything started out fine, but the plans for the new house kept changing, and it got out of hand. Wally wanted to live in an elaborate home on the golf course, but it felt wrong to Loretta. She didn't think God had spared her life to be some person living in a fancy house. She had other responsibilities.

Construction had been underway for more than a year, but Loretta wasn't happy about it, not like she was when they built their first house in Sycamore. Back then, Loretta had contributed to every detail and couldn't wait to pick out every little thing, down to the baseboards and switch plates. Now she didn't want to pick out anything. She didn't even want to go in it.

Ultimately, that house became her ball and chain. The closer it got to being finished, the less she wanted to live there. "It was a total lie. And then Wally was angry with me about that and said, 'Why didn't you say something when the hole was dug?' Well, I didn't know how to stop it."

They never did move in.

When Loretta thought about it, she knew the house wasn't the real problem. There were other issues they hadn't faced that had layered one on top of the other until it felt like all they had were problems. Mainly, she felt inadequate in their relationship, like she had dropped the ball and was no longer pulling her weight.

"I was no longer taking care of my part of the 'Wally and Loretta world.' I never felt like an equal again, and I resented that. Wally made me feel like a child, and in some ways, he was an overprotective parent. I couldn't do this or that because he was too worried about me. It was *smothering*. I was no longer a wife; I was a patient, and Wally was my caregiver. I felt like I'd been erased."

Suffocating in her situation, Loretta needed to find herself again. She had to know that the person she used to be was still in there. Her former life had been snatched from her, and although she had learned to do many things by herself, she'd been scarred by her dependency. She needed to learn that the heart and soul of the true Loretta was still in one piece. More than anything, she needed to re-bloom. For that, she needed space.

Friends in the neighborhood told Wally in retrospect, "You were too cautious for her. You should have let her be, let her do, let her try." If it had been up to Wally, she felt sure she would have never ridden a bike, or jumped on a trampoline, or taken off her legs and swam across the pool.

"But that's really not fair to him. I felt like he was holding me back, but I wasn't strong enough to tell him what I wanted, so he didn't know. I can't blame Wally. We were in a crisis, and he had to step up and take control, but when I was capable again, I needed him to turn some of that back over to me. But I never asked for it. I just expected him to know. I kept thinking, *How can you not know?*

"I should have told him how I felt."

At the same time she felt controlled by Wally, Loretta was also indebted to him because he did so much for her, which is why she didn't think she should voice her frustrations. So her resentments did what all unresolved resentments do: they festered and grew.

All she heard about was how wonderful Wally was. Even her sisters said, "Wally was there for you. You don't know what he went through when you were on life support." Others suggested that Wally could have left her because that's what some people do: they leave if things aren't perfect.

When she was in the hospital, the nurses told her about a patient who had been flown in from Florida. Her husband left her because she had meningitis and was going to lose a limb. Loretta thought, *Okay, Wally did a lot, but would someone really leave just because you got sick? Who does that kind of thing?* She knew she should be grateful, but her feelings didn't square up. She would cry and say to God, *Please don't be disappointed in me, but I'm frustrated, and I'm angry, and I'm sad.*

"It was so, so hard. I just couldn't be me. No one was allowing me to be me or to find me, and I couldn't communicate all that frustration about Wally because everyone thought Wally was fabulous."

Loretta's feelings were real, and they were strong. Did she imagine that Wally thought she was a burden because of her own need to be independent, her own need to know that she could still function? Possibly. But over time, a wall built up between them, and after awhile she couldn't see past it.

Loretta talked to their pastor about their problems, and later, Wally joined her. But because of their unique situation, the pastor thought they should see someone who had more training.

When they finally went to a professional counselor, Wally said, "I'm just doing what I did before when we built the house in Sycamore. I went to work, and then I worked on the new house when I was off. And that's what I'm doing now. Loretta's never said anything about being unhappy. She hasn't complained."

Wally was right. He was doing exactly what he had done before, except this time Loretta saw a drastic difference. When they were building their house in Sycamore, Wally went to work and then went to the new house, and Loretta was also busy doing her part, which was taking care of their new baby. Now they were building another house, but this time, Loretta was the one being cared for. She felt like she was the baby.

There were no villains here. What happened to Loretta was horrendous, but what Wally went through was also dreadful. "I can't imagine being the spouse on the other side of the situation," Loretta said.

"We were both changed forever."

Chapter 20

Wally and Loretta tried some last-ditch marriage counseling, but in the end, it didn't seem to make much difference. The trauma of the past several years had been too much, and it wrenched them apart. People on the outside would say, "This should have brought you so much closer," or "You survived all of that and lived through hell on earth together," but the truth was, they no longer shared common goals, and their vision for the future didn't match. After much deliberation, they decided to divorce in October 2008, three years after they moved to Edwardsville.

To keep it simple, they used the same attorney and went to all the appointments together. Everything was split 50/50, which was the typical way that Wally and Loretta handled things. When the divorce was final, they didn't need to go to court; they just signed the papers in his office and went their separate ways.

During that time, Loretta couldn't help but think about Heather Mills. She and Paul McCartney had divorced a couple of years earlier, and she wondered how Heather had held up against all the awful things that had been written and said about her. Loretta had seen the tabloids and knew they'd gotten it all wrong.

"Heather was always warm and approachable, and just a delightful woman to be around. She was not the person the papers in England made her out to be. She's not a gold digger, and she's not hard-hearted. This lovely, down-to-earth woman took time out of her busy schedule to take care of this one little woman who needed help, and we became friends. For me, everything Heather did just accentuated how lovely she is. She befriended me, she gave me confidence and hope, and she certainly didn't have to go out of her way like she did. Heather was my real-life example of an amputee who was still glamorous and pretty and getting around just fine."

After she signed the divorce papers, Loretta left the attorney's office. It hadn't felt traumatic, like she thought it might. She went shopping and bought herself a handbag, then she called her mom.

"Do you think that's bad? We just signed the papers, and I went out and bought a purse."

"No," Wanda answered. "You were just trying to take your mind off of everything."

The emotions hit later.

Loretta and Wally had stayed under the same roof until it was time to finalize the divorce, but a few days beforehand, Wally said, "If we sign the paperwork on Friday, I think you should move out on Saturday."

They had eventually purchased the house that they were renting, and Wally got to keep it. The attorney thought Loretta was nuts to give it up, but she said, "I don't want to live there. It's not Loretta-friendly, it has steps down to the family room, and there are too many things about it that annoy me. And Wally is a person who fares better if he has projects to do, and that's a project home. He's a golfer, and the golf course is in the backyard. I have friends all over town, but most of Wally's friends are his golf friends who live in that neighborhood." So Loretta moved out.

She had to find a place to live, and for some reason, her friend Becky kept coming to mind. She met Becky at Mitch's very first soccer game, shortly after they moved to Edwardsville. Loretta was new in town then and didn't exactly know where she was going that day. She parked at one end of the street and saw another blonde mom who drove the same kind of silver SUV parked at the other end. Loretta called out, "I like your car! We're bookends!" She and Becky had been friends ever since. Over the years, they'd both gotten so busy that they could usually only get together for their birthdays, so she didn't get to see Becky very often.

But now she had this nagging feeling that she should call her about finding a house. Come to find out, Becky had just gotten married and had moved in with her new husband. Becky's house was for sale, and when she moved out, she hadn't taken any of her furniture or dishes—everything was still in place. It was the perfect setup for Loretta, and Becky knew she would keep it neat, so the realtor could show it. She was delighted to have Loretta move in.

"The house didn't really need anything, but I went to Target and bought new flannel sheets for all the beds, and Mitch and Alyssa went with me. Alyssa was Miss Queen Bee and helped me take care of everything, but when we got to the house, Mitch went in, walked around the house, walked back out, and sat out in the car. He didn't want to live there."

She knew that moving again would be hard for everyone, but had always thought that her children would live with her. That didn't happen. Their roots were in the other house, so they stayed with Wally because they didn't want to move out of their rooms.

She never lived with her children again.

But Loretta didn't feel like she had "lost" her kids because she spent every day at the old house doing what she'd always done—being the mom. Wally was at work, so he didn't mind. She was there when Mitch and Alyssa got home from school. She bought all the groceries and baked cookies. She cleaned the floors and scrubbed the bathrooms. Loretta did everything she'd always done with one exception: She didn't sleep under that roof.

"But it exhausted me to take care of two households. I was over there cleaning all the time, and my family could see it was wearing me out. 'Loretta, please, you've got to quit,' they said. But these were my children, and I wanted to take care of them. I was still their mom. I wasn't going to give that up."

On the weekends, Alyssa liked to go to Loretta's house to spend the night, especially with her girlfriends. But not Mitch. Mitch never stayed overnight.

The divorce was final at the end of October, and then came the holidays. Of course, Loretta wanted to keep everything the same for the kids. They had always spent Thanksgiving with her side of the family, and since the kids were with her that year, too, it all seemed normal. But Christmas was a little more challenging. Loretta did all the Christmas shopping and wrapped all the gifts in the basement at Wally's house, as usual. On Christmas Eve, she drove over there and went to church with the kids, and when they got back, she prepared all their traditional Christmas recipes, like the overnight egg casserole and French toast. Then she got in her car and drove home.

On Christmas morning, Loretta got up early and stayed in her pajamas.

She packed some clothes to change into later and was back at Wally's house around five or five-thirty. They carried the gifts up from the basement, so that when the kids woke up, it would seem like a normal Christmas. But it wasn't really the same because when Mitch and Alyssa got up, their parents were sitting in their pajamas at complete opposite ends of the couch watching *The Little Rascals.* They'd never seen anything like that before.

Life goes on, even when it changes.

PART FOUR

My Whole
Soul Smiles

There is no exercise better for the heart than reaching down and lifting people up.

~ John Andrew Holmes

Chapter 21

Loretta had always been fastidious about her grooming, and after suffering so many physical losses, she was even more determined to keep up her appearance. She made an appointment for a facial and arrived at Dutch Hollow Medical Day Spa in Godfrey, Illinois, wearing her glamour legs and high heels—with perfectly polished toenails—and her prosthetic hand. She walked through the door and entered the life of Mirka Figueroa, the spa owner.

Mirka seated Loretta in a comfortable chair for her pre-treatment consultation. "This procedure also includes a massage for your hands and feet," she said.

"That sounds nice, but I don't have any," Loretta said.

Mirka was puzzled. She had emigrated from Poland thirty years before, and even though English is her second language, she is quite fluent. However, on occasion, she still came across an occasional nuance or phrase that she didn't quite understand.

"I don't know what you mean," Mirka said.

"I mean that I don't have any feet and only part of one hand," Loretta said. She told Mirka the whole story about her injury and subsequent amputations.

Mirka was stunned. "I didn't know what to say. I could hardly believe what this beautiful, vibrant woman told me. Not only did she survive a near-death experience, but she had to deal with the aftermath of the amputations. And then she walks into my spa with no apparent handicaps. I would have never guessed!

"Afterward, I just couldn't stop thinking about her," she said. "Loretta made me realize how important it is to enjoy every day. I knew her story would change people's lives. By her example, she can help others learn how to stay positive and to handle anything that comes their way. Loretta came through an incredible trial, and *everyone* can learn *something* from her."

The two became close friends, and Mirka says that because of Loretta, she now looks at her own life through a completely different lens. Loretta made her realize that the ordinary problems people worry about don't seem nearly as important when they're put in perspective. "And I don't think it's a coincidence that Loretta and I were brought together. Before I opened my spa, I was a physical therapist who worked with amputees."

Mirka remembered those amputees and was amazed at the distinct difference in Loretta. "I've seen people have a very hard time adapting to the loss of just one limb, let alone both legs, a hand, and most of her other fingers. So many amputees get terribly depressed and feel sorry for themselves, which I understand. But Loretta's not that way. When she walks in the room, you can literally feel her positive attitude, and that causes others to consider their own lives in a new light. And it doesn't only apply to those who have lost a limb. Any illness or difficult circumstance can be improved by having a positive outlook."

"Sometimes when I've overdone it," Loretta told Mirka, "or if my legs hurt, or if I've lifted a case of water into the grocery cart, it gets hard. But I am determined to keep going and to do the things that I want and need to do."

"You have no idea how you could impact people," Mirka told her. "I'm having an open house at the spa in a couple of weeks. Would you consider being a guest speaker? I would love for you to tell your story. A lot of people could benefit from what you have to say."

Loretta agreed, and the next thing she knew, she was speaking to a crowd of about two hundred at Dutch Hollow. She told them how on an ordinary day, her life was turned upside down when she hit her hand on the banister.

"Life does go on, even when you don't see how it possibly can, and there's a positive way to view whatever comes along," she told them. "No matter what problems or challenges you encounter, don't ever let them prevent you from living life to the fullest.

"I never dreamed I could withstand a life-threatening illness and the loss of my limbs—and then go back to being the happy person I had always been.

Of course, it takes a while to heal emotionally from any sickness or loss, but then there comes a time when you have to get over it and go back to living, with adjustments certainly, but you can't give up on life and hide at home all the time."

Instead of focusing on what was taken from her, Loretta told them that she focuses on the gift she was given: Life.

"My doctor told me that ninety percent of people who have severe strep toxic shock die, but I'm still alive," she said. "There's a reason I survived, and it wasn't to sit around and feel sorry for myself, but to go on and be the person I was meant to be. Around the fifth anniversary of my illness, I did a lot of reflecting and realized that if you can't embrace who you are, then you're the only one who can change it.

"I've never done the 'could haves, should haves, would haves.' You can drive yourself crazy with questions like, *What if I hadn't been home that day? What if I was upstairs when the doorbell rang? What if the UPS man had skipped my house?* But that's a waste of time. You can get stuck in that kind of cycle, and it's not healthy. No, you just take the day and move on to the next and learn from it. You can revisit it later if you want to reflect, but not to beat yourself up or wrestle with regrets. It's just not productive."

Loretta talked about the changes that had taken place within her, and how she could look in the mirror again without feeling sad because she's accepted the new normal. "And what kind of life would I have if I didn't accept it? I would be unhappy, my friends and family probably wouldn't want to be around me if all I did was complain—and it still wouldn't change what happened. I would still be an amputee.

"Parts is parts, and I'm still me," she said. "Do I still love myself? You bet I do. That's the first step. You have to care about yourself and take care of your inner life, as well as your outward self."

In fact, Loretta does such a good job that most people don't know she has a disability. She told the audience about the night she took her kids and some of their neighborhood friends downtown to see the Halloween parade. They parked in a handicapped spot, which Loretta affectionately calls "celebrity parking," and when they got out of the car, a brusque woman started cursing at her.

She tried to tell the woman that it was perfectly legitimate for her to park in a handicapped spot, but the woman wouldn't listen. Loretta said she was a bilateral amputee and even twisted her prosthetic hand around backward to prove it, but the woman kept on shouting. "I guess she thought the hand was a Halloween prop, because she didn't stop yelling," Loretta laughed.

On occasion when Loretta is pumping gas, someone notices her missing fingers and asks if they can help her. "I just smile and say, 'Thank you, but I'm fine.' Often, their curiosity gets the best of them, and they want to know what happened to my hand, which opens up the whole story. I've made several friends that way."

When she finished speaking, the audience sat silent for a few moments, then broke into applause. Loretta was eager to answer their questions.

"Were you ever mad at God?" one woman asked.

"No, I wasn't mad at God. He was in my story all along," she said. "If he wasn't, I wouldn't be here. Every time I needed something, he would put the right person in the right place at the right time, like when Heather Mills called me at the exact moment I needed her. And I feel like my life is exactly what it was meant to be," she said. "God gave me the strength, the personality type, and the people who helped me and encouraged me to figure things out. He's been guiding me the entire way."

"Don't you have down times?" someone else asked.

"There are still days when I feel down, and I still have bad leg days. I've fallen down a few times and landed on my knees. But you just get back up and go on. One time when I was trying to get in my car, my whole leg fell off in the parking lot! So I just hung onto the car door, picked it up, reattached it, and went on my way. What else can you do?" she asked.

"I have the best prosthetics that are available, and even though I live a full life, it can still be really difficult. It's a daily struggle, but I try to take it in stride."

After the event, Loretta received several notes from audience members. She read through the messages, one by one. "It was so heartwarming," she said. "I could literally feel the emotion and love in that room. I think my story made a difference to people, and for the first time since this whole tragedy began, I honestly felt my whole soul smile. That night I discovered my purpose—to be an inspiration every single day, to use my experiences and my continuing challenges to help others through difficult situations."

The note from an eleven-year-old girl was particularly touching.

> *Loretta,*
>   *I think you are so amazing. I have never met*
> *anyone with so much heart and determination in*
> *my life. Even though I'm only eleven years old, you*
> *are an inspiration forever.*
>   *Sincerely,*
>   *Maegan Vinson*

Loretta was eager to spread her story of hope and encouragement and speak at other venues, but she stumbled on one point. Other than the evening at Dutch Hollow, she had no public speaking experience. What if she couldn't do it? What if she couldn't connect with a broader audience?

She had a friend whose husband was in Toastmasters, the international public speaking organization, who suggested that Loretta speak at one of the meetings to get their input. "I don't know if I want to do that," she protested. "Some of them have been involved in public speaking for fifty years."

And yet, it sounded like the perfect audience to give her credible feedback, so she agreed to appear as a guest speaker. Loretta didn't want anyone to see her beforehand, so she stayed hidden in a small room while her friend introduced her.

"Our guest speaker is a woman who would like to get more experience speaking in public, and she asked to come here tonight to get some practice. We want you to critique her and to be brutally honest," she said. "She wants to improve, so be tough."

Loretta walked in and greeted everyone. They gave her a warm welcome, but she felt intimidated to stand at the front of the room with only a chair and a table to keep her company. "In fact, I was a wreck. I was so nervous, I felt like I was taking a final exam. There were all these business-looking people, and they were sitting in a semi-circle with their legal pads and pens. And I had no clue what they were writing down. To me, the speech went pretty well. I didn't say 'um' or any of those fillers. I just spoke and didn't use note cards or props. I walked up and down at the front of the room and spoke directly to each person at some point, but the whole time I kept thinking, *What are they writing?*"

She started her story on December 11, 2001, and told them that prior to that date, she was an average stay-at-home mom. She continued with the story until she reached the point where she had the amputations. Loretta was wearing Capri pants and high-heeled sandals that evening, and as she spoke, the audience looked at her like, *Why is she talking about leg amputations when she's standing right in front of us?*

She told them about her hair coming out in handfuls and the marks on her mouth from the life support, as well as the scars on her side where they drained the infection. She held out her right hand to show that she had lost her fingers.

"Then I pulled off my left hand. I sat down in the chair and made eye contact with each of them. They began shifting in their seats, like, *Oh my gosh, I've been watching her for the last forty minutes and I had no clue about that hand—and there it is, lying on the table.*

"Then I pulled off both legs, and set them to the side."

The audience was stunned into silence. Here she was, "Loretta in the Rough." She smiled and looked around the room and swung her short little legs back and forth like a child who can't quite reach the floor. Her left hand was on the table, as lifeless as a rubber glove, but her face was radiant. She looked so innocent, it was heartbreaking.

"I was sitting there thinking back over my speech. What did I say, or what was I doing with my body language that made them start making notes on their legal pads? There were a lot of mental things going on at once, and when you speak to a small group and see true emotion, it's a little unsettling."

Suddenly, the silence broke. The audience cried, laughed, clapped—and they erupted from their chairs.

Afterward, one of the men approached her.

"I love your hands," he said. "They're touching more people now than the ones you were born with."

Chapter 22

For Loretta, the best part of living in Edwardsville was being near her parents and sisters, and they made a point to get together for both large and small events. "Now that you live close to us," Lola said, "you can be part of our family garage sale." Loretta rolled her eyes at her sister and groaned. Garage sales weren't her thing, but her sisters had one every spring.

"Your house is in such a good location," Lola added. "Could we have it there?"

"Of course," Loretta said. "I would love that."

As the date got closer, she thought about what she could contribute to the sale. She still had boxes that she'd never unpacked from their move from Sycamore, and that was years ago. As she sorted through the pile, she found some clothes the kids had outgrown, a few pairs of shoes that still looked like new, and something else, something she hadn't thought about in a very long time. It was the blanket her friend had given her right after her legs were amputated. She'd used it as a lap blanket when she sat in the recliner in the playroom. *It was nice to have that when I needed so much comfort, but maybe someone else can use it now,* she thought. She placed it in the basket of things she needed to wash for the sale.

After the blanket was washed, she smoothed it out and read the poem that was embroidered into the fabric. Those words had been a source of strength and consolation during some of her darkest days.

I said a prayer for you today and know God must have heard;
I felt the answer in my heart although he spoke no word.
I didn't ask for wealth or fame. I knew you wouldn't mind.
I asked him to send treasures of a far more lasting kind.
I asked that he'd be near you at the start of each new day
To grant you health and blessings and friends to share the way.

On the day of the sale, Loretta showed it to her sisters. "I remember that blanket," Laura said. "Are you sure you don't want to keep it?"

"I don't think so," she said. "It really helped me at the time, but I think it's time to pass it on."

That afternoon, Paula Gallagher spotted the blanket. It looked warm and comfortable, and she thought it might be something that would help her father, Dave Diestelhorst, who had recently lost his left leg in a tractor accident. When she read the message, she knew she was right. The blanket would be perfect for him.

It was a beautiful spring day, although still a bit chilly, and Loretta had slipped inside to make hot chocolate for everyone. Lola noticed Paula handling the blanket and could tell that she was interested. "That's a special blanket," she told her.

"I was thinking it would be nice for my dad. He had a terrible accident and just had his leg amputated. I wanted to find something cozy for him," Paula answered.

"I'm so sorry to hear that," Lola said, "but you aren't going to believe this. My sister is the one who is selling it, and someone gave her that blanket when she had both of her legs amputated." Lola told her the whole story of Loretta's illness and recovery.

"Then it was meant to be," Paula said, her eyes full of tears. She bought the blanket and left thinking about Loretta.

"Dad," she said when she got to the rehab center, "I have something for you. This blanket will keep you warm, and I think it's meant just for you. You won't believe where it came from." She told him about the garage sale and what she'd heard about Loretta, then placed the blanket across his lap and read the poem aloud. It seemed to provide him immediate warmth and relief, and he snuggled underneath it and fell into a restful sleep.

Dave was released from rehab a few weeks later, but by fall, it was obvious that he was not adjusting well to life without his leg. He sat inside all day and wouldn't try to do anything for himself. He had been an over-the-road truck driver for forty years, but at sixty-nine, he was now retired. Always active and eager to help others, Dave, in typical fashion, had been helping his neighbor mow the yard when the accident occurred. He was climbing up on the tractor in the light rain when he lost his footing and slipped. He fell under the tire and was immediately pulled into the mower. His left leg was so mangled that it had to be amputated above the knee. The recovery was long and difficult, and he just couldn't accept the change.

Paula remembered the story about Loretta. *I wonder if she could help,* she thought. *Maybe if Dad saw how well she's handling her amputations, it would inspire him.*

But there was a problem: Paula didn't know how to find Loretta. She remembered the street where the yard sale had been, but she couldn't recall the exact address, so she drove around thinking she could find the house, but that didn't work. She couldn't remember what it looked like.

Soon after, Paula was talking to her cousin and mentioned that she was trying to find the woman who had sold her the blanket. She re-told the story she'd heard about Loretta, and as she did so, her cousin interrupted. "Wait! I think I know who she is. I don't know her personally, but that has to be my friend Lola's sister. There can't be more than one woman in this small community with a story like that," she said.

They got in touch with Lola, who called Loretta right away. "The lady who bought your blanket is trying to find you," Lola said. "She wants to know if you would talk to her father. He's having a hard time with his amputation."

"Absolutely," Loretta said. "I would love to meet him. I don't know what I would have done if I hadn't had Heather in my life, and I plan to be there for other people, like she was for me. Give me his number, and I'll call right now."

Dave's wife, Jane, answered and said, "We just don't know what to do. He's depressed and isn't handling the situation well. I thought that if he could meet someone who has experienced the same thing, he would see that he can still live a full life, too."

They scheduled a visit, and Loretta thought long and hard about how she could bring a little joy back into Dave's life. She picked up a nice plant and went to the bakery to buy a big cookie, and asked them to write "Because I Understand" across the top in icing. She wanted Dave to know that she knew exactly what he was feeling.

When the two met, they both started to cry. Dave, who had been sitting in his house, dark and morose for nearly a year, lit up when he saw how confident and radiant Loretta, an amputee like himself, was. At that moment they bonded, and they both knew in their hearts that it was no accident that they had found each other.

Loretta told Dave what happened to her, and that when she saw for herself how Heather Mills had gone on with her life, she realized that she could—and must—do the same. "I drive and do almost everything I did before," she said. "It took a while for me to learn, but you can do it, too. Just think, you only lost one leg, and since you still have your right one, I know you can drive."

Dave didn't like the way his prosthetic leg felt, and Loretta told him that he didn't have to settle for a leg that didn't fit. She visited often to give him pointers about how to adapt to life while wearing an artificial leg.

"You have to establish a new center of gravity," she told him, "and it's important to get some exercise. You can do sit ups, lift hand weights, and do leg lifts—anything that strengthens your stomach and leg muscles will help you with your balance."

Walking on the new leg was physically hard on Dave. Since his leg had been amputated above the knee, he had some obstacles to overcome that below-the-knee amputees don't face. His prosthesis had a knee joint, which had to bend and flex without buckling when he walked. The artificial joint made it hard to walk with a natural, balanced gait, and Dave had to devote both time and energy to practice. Loretta was fortunate that she still had both her own knees, but she also knew there were many above-the-knee amputees who had learned to walk again. She was determined to help Dave however she could, and through her encouragement, he seemed to feel a little more positive.

"Practice makes perfect," she told him, "and you should see what I've had to learn because I lost a hand and all my fingers, too. Some things that seemed impossible in the beginning aren't a problem now because I practiced until I could do it."

She gave him dozens of examples of how she had invented ways to do things on her own. At first, she didn't want to use anything that came in a can unless it had a pop-top, but even that was difficult. "Let's say I need to open a can of soup. I don't have a finger to put in the pop-top, so I hold the can close to my body and stick a knife in the loop and pop it up. Then I put it down on the counter and slowly pull off the lid with the knife.

"And I don't like to get gas. Just doing the credit card thing can be bad because when the card goes in too far, I can't get at it to pull it back out. So I worry that I'll have to ask the person next to me to get my card out. And I won't even tell you how hard it can be to get the gas cap off. Despite all that, I pump my own gas because I will not allow myself to be at the mercy of others.

"Coins and I don't get along so well either," she continued, "but that's another thing. Thank goodness for debit cards, because if anyone hands me change and I drop it—well forget it. I can't pick it up. The point is, if there's something you want to do, then figure out how to do it, or find another way."

Loretta kept pestering Dave to drive, and she brought it up nearly every time they talked. She would say, "Dave, you have one good leg and you should get behind the wheel and use it," and she even volunteered to go with him while he learned. One day, he decided to give it a try, but it didn't go well. He kept veering off the side of the road, and he finally pulled over and said, "I can't do this anymore."

Dave often talked about how much Loretta meant to him and how she helped with his recovery. "I can't explain it, but Loretta helped me a lot," he said. "She always came in with a smile on her face, and that gave me encouragement. She is never down in the dumps.

"I'm just an old truck driver. I drove six million miles during my career," he said. "But I would have sat back and felt sorry for myself, if it weren't for her. I don't think I would have recovered as well as I did without Loretta. I always look forward to seeing her. She's a remarkable and extraordinary lady, and she's like another daughter to me."

Dave's family did their part to boost his spirits, and since Loretta had essentially become part of their family, they invited her to come to a "Just Because" party they were giving in his honor. The party was going well, but after a while, Dave became really agitated. He was nervous and upset because the children were running around, and he wasn't used to all the noise and commotion. Loretta saw he was getting disturbed, and she intervened. She sat down with him and told him to relax, and he soon composed himself. Dave loved Loretta, and she had an amazing ability to soothe him when no one else could.

On November 18, 2008, Dave died from an infection. He left behind five daughters, two sons, twenty-two grandchildren, and twenty-six great-grandchildren. He is buried just outside of Bunker Hill, in the same cemetery where Loretta's grandparents are buried. She visits his grave frequently and talks to him about the pain in her legs, speaking amputee-to-amputee. "I miss him. I became so close to Dave and his wife that I called them Mom and Dad," she said. "We had a real bond."

Loretta is convinced that her life was spared so she could help people like Dave, and that being an amputee is part and parcel of that. "My relationship with Dave is another example of how God provided exactly what was needed at the exact right time. Dave needed someone who understood his pain, and I needed someone to encourage. I will never forget him," she said.

Loretta reaches out to people with all sorts of physical challenges, and when she connects with fellow amputees, particularly those who are having a hard time adjusting, she finds they have so many questions—about her recovery, about her prosthetics, and most of all, about her positive attitude and how she accepted her new way of life. She wants to be an example, to show them that life goes on, and that they can ultimately choose to be positive about anything that comes their way.

Sometimes people approach her directly, and at other times, her doctors or the staff at Dorset or other support organizations ask her to reach out to someone who is struggling. One time when she was back in Chicago, Loretta ran into one of her original doctors who hadn't seen her since the amputations. All he could say was, "Wow!" She told him about everything she could do again, and assured him that her life had not been slowed down by her situation. He immediately asked her to be a peer buddy for those with similar circumstances.

Loretta didn't even pause. "Of course I will," she said. "Just tell me who, when, and where."

Chapter 23

It was a crisp December morning, and Loretta went to Sam's Club with a friend to shop for food and the other items they needed for their holiday entertaining. They loaded up the trunk and left, but as they exited the parking lot, the car seemed to be off balance. Her friend got out to take a look and, greeted by the distinct hiss of a leaking tire, suggested they go back to the auto center to get it fixed.

A string of customers were ahead of them and, knowing it would be a long wait, they went back in the store to wander around. After a few aisles, Loretta got tired and went back to sit down.

"Excuse me, sir," she asked the fifty-something man who was sitting on the bench. "Would you mind sharing this seat with me?"

He scooted over and Loretta sat down. "I'm sorry, but I'm an amputee, and I need to pop my leg off because it hurts so bad. We've been walking around the store too long," she explained.

"You're an amputee?" he asked. "I'm having my leg removed the day after tomorrow. Diabetes."

Loretta immediately offered words of encouragement, and he told her that he was upset because they wanted to amputate higher than he thought was necessary.

"I think that taking the foot is enough," he said.

"My doctor told me the same thing," she said, "and I argued that I wanted to keep as much of my leg as I could, but he said that if they amputated higher, it would be easier for me to walk with prosthetics because my balance would be better. I didn't want to hear that, but now that it's behind me, I know he was right."

That thought soaked in for a minute, and then he responded. "When you walked over here, I would never have guessed that both of your legs had been amputated. I'm glad I got to talk to you."

The man's car was ready, and Loretta wished him well. They didn't exchange phone numbers, and she'd probably never know how he fared following his operation, but after he left, Loretta felt like what she told him had made a difference, that it had better prepared him for what he was about to face. She knew that meeting him was no coincidence, and she marveled at how many similar situations she'd experienced. If she hadn't had a problem with her tire, hadn't walked around too long, or had come in a few minutes later, she never would have met this man. She was meant to be at that specific place at that precise time, so she could encourage him and offer help in her own small way.

During her recovery and the ensuing years, Loretta often knelt down on her bare knees and prayed, *Lord, give me the tenacity of a weed.* Of course, nobody loves weeds. Weeds aren't pretty, they're scrappy, and there's always someone or something out to destroy them. And yet, weeds are incredibly resilient. They keep popping up, no matter what. *Lord, give me the tenacity of a weed.*

"I was pruned down to Loretta in the Rough and I needed to re-bloom," she tells other sufferers, "and I prayed for the strength to do that."

Loretta is convinced that she survived because she was healthy, strong, and physically fit before she hit her hand. "If I hadn't been so fit, I don't think there's any way I could have held up against the strep infection." After she recovered, it was even more important for her to exercise and eat right. Although she could have easily succumbed to self-pity and depression, she kept pushing ahead and never stopped strengthening her body, before and after her amputations. She wanted to look good and feel good about herself, and she was determined that her jeans and other clothes would fit her just like they always had.

Whatever her motivation, she was tenacious about exercise, even during her darkest moments. Every January, she made New Year's resolutions, and in 2007, she set the nearly impossible goal of riding 3,650 miles on her stationary bike, an average of ten miles a day. She made a plan for the entire year and tried to ride first thing every morning.

At times, her family commitments made it difficult to stay on track, and by August, she faced a 390-mile deficit. Rather than sink under the struggle, she forged ahead. Between September 1 and December 19, she added a few extra miles to her daily quota, got back on target, and by December 31, Loretta had reached her goal—3,650 miles.

"Riding is a mental thing," she said, "and I won't ever stop. It takes me places when I ride, and I do a lot of reflecting." She has an eclectic taste in music, and Josh Groban is one of her favorite artists to listen to during her long rides, although she likes to mix it up with Tina Turner, Prince, Aerosmith, and Celine Dion. "So many of the songs take me back to a different time. When I ride, I do some soul-searching and thinking," she said. "I close my eyes and sort of dream. In my mind, I see myself as I was before. I have legs, and I'm flying."

Loretta nosed her SUV into the celebrity parking space at the grocery store. She strolled in, grabbed a cart, and waved at Judy, the floral manager, as she walked past the spring displays nestled in brightly colored pots.

"Hi Lee," she called to the man stocking rows of ground beef in the meat department. "You getting ready to go on your trip?"

"I'm leaving Saturday and can't wait. Thanks for asking," he replied.

Loretta knew almost everyone who worked in the store by name. She shopped two or three times a week and always took the time to stop and chat. Today she had a long list. Alyssa was having a slumber party at her house, and she needed a few things to make one of her favorite dishes for dinner—Cajun Chicken Pasta. She also wanted to stock the pantry with fun snacks and to fill the fridge with an assortment of bottled water, juices, and soft drinks.

She turned the cart into the beverage aisle and saw a woman in her forties coming toward her. She was in a wheelchair, and both legs ended about mid calf, just like Loretta's. The woman was wearing liners, so Loretta knew she had artificial limbs, but for some reason, she didn't have them on. Another woman, who Loretta assumed was her daughter, walked next to her and was pushing a stroller that had a napping baby inside.

"We match," Loretta said to the woman in the wheelchair.

"What do you mean?" she asked, a puzzled look on her face. "Do I know you?"

"No, but my name is Loretta, and I wanted to show you that our legs are exactly the same." She hung onto the grocery shelf, lifted her pant leg, and popped off one of her legs, which promptly fell over into the aisle. "I have another one just like it," she said.

The woman looked confused, but then broke into a smile.

"I would have never thought you were wearing prosthetics," she said. "You walk so well. I just can't do it."

"Now I have to sit on your lap to put this back on," Loretta said.

The woman drew back in astonishment.

"I'm just kidding," Loretta said, laughing. "I can get it back on." She bent over, picked up her leg, and popped it back on while she leaned against the shelf.

"You've given me hope," the woman said to her. "I wasn't sure anyone could really walk in prosthetics."

Fifteen minutes later, they saw each other again when they were checking out, and their paths crossed a third time near the exit doors.

"I've been thinking," the woman said. "If you can walk the way you do, then I can, too. I'm going to learn to walk again for my grandbaby." She nodded toward the infant in the stroller.

"Good for you," Loretta said. "You'll need to be on your feet, because you're going to have a tiny hiney to chase before long."

Epilogue

Life goes on ...

Loretta hit her hand on December 11, 2001, and since that time, her family has gone through countless changes—both good and bad. Mitch and Alyssa are older now, and they remain very close to her. She still loves to spend time with them and their friends.

Wally and Loretta's marriage was yet one more casualty of the obtrusive strep germ that lurked on Loretta's skin and invaded her life. Navigating disaster is a wild ride, and the people involved can emerge from such tragedies only to discover they have a different outlook and a different perspective on life, and they often find their partner is different, too. In some ways, Loretta and Wally are still on the same page, at least as far as their children are concerned. Together, they guided them into adulthood, and both are always attentive to Mitch and Alyssa. They even took several college-hunting trips together with each of them, and they remain an active part of their lives.

They always will be.

Loretta's illness changed her life in so many ways, but she works hard to keep the important things the same. Her sense of humor, her faith, her family and friends, and her quest to make all things Loretta-friendly are still the status quo. It will always take extra effort for her to do things that were once elementary. She still begins and ends her days on her knees. That's a fact of her life.

Once a homebody, she's now a motivational speaker, and her engagements often take her on the road to churches, universities, high schools, veteran's hospitals, conferences, and even larger venues. And that's okay with her. Her goal is to spread hope and inspiration. She wants to broadcast what she's learned: That no matter how bad the circumstances seem on the surface, if you learn to go with the flow and don't take yourself too seriously, it can mean the difference between acceptance and despair. Before she parts with her audience, Loretta leaves them with this final thought:

> *My message is not just for amputees. Everyone suffers at some point, whether it's through a chronic illness, the loss of a job, a death, a divorce, or even the daily problems that pile up and seem insurmountable. We all feel sorry for ourselves at times. But if I had given in to my overwhelming emotions or my physical limitations, it would have been like having another amputation. I would have been the loser—again. I had to fight and push, and I couldn't let my circumstances define me.*
>
> *I want to help other people face their own challenges, whatever they are, in that same way.*
>
> *I want to be someone's Heather.*

Photo Gallery

*Most of the photos in this Gallery are family snapshots that are difficult
to reproduce for print. The color photos may be viewed at www.ALifeInParts.com.*

The Goebel's house in Sycamore, Illinois.

Loretta Goebel before.

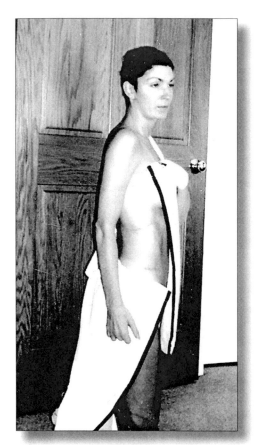

Loretta Goebel after, standing.

Mitch celebrates his tenth birthday at the hospital.

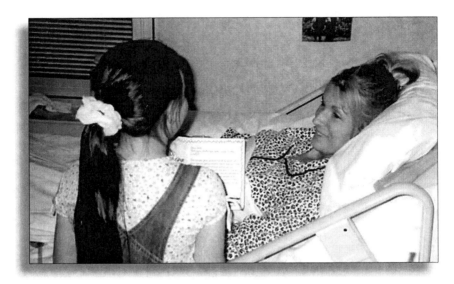

Alyssa reads get well cards to her mother.

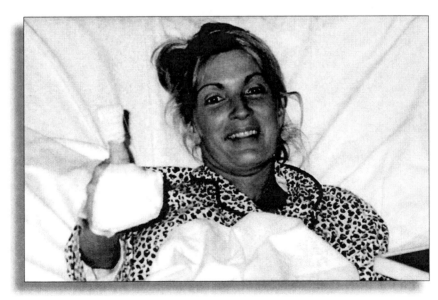

Loretta gives her signature 'thumbs up.'

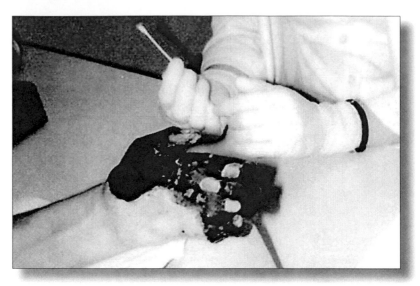

Loretta's left hand before it was amputated.

Loretta with Mitch and Alyssa. Her hands are bandaged
and she is wearing her Barbie wig and her first set of legs.

Her fingers have been amputated,
and she is still wearing the
'bubble legs.'

Loretta can still keep the
hula hoops going,
even with her big legs.

193

Photo of Heather Mills that started them on their search for 'glamour' legs.

Dorset Orthopaedic, where Heather Mills' and Loretta's legs were manufactured.

Loretta with Paul McCartney after his concert in Chicago.

Bob and Tessa Watts of Dorset Orthopaedic Co., Ltd.

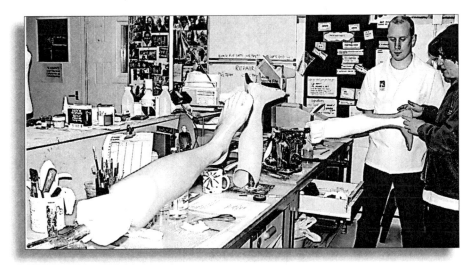

Dorset technicians painstakingly create lifelike limbs.

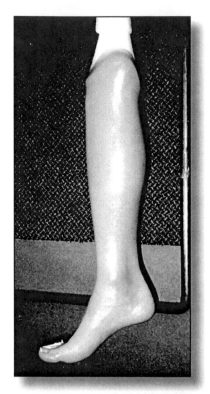

A Dorset leg.

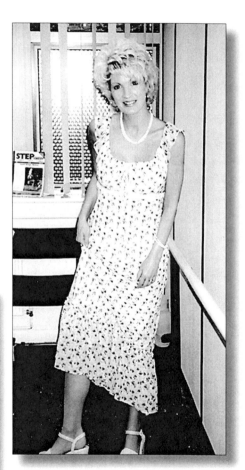

Loretta tries out her first
set of Dorset legs.

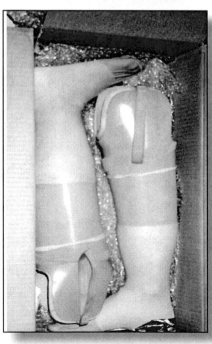

Loretta's 'bubble' legs,
boxed up and ready to
send to Heather Mills.

Heather and Loretta, wearing their matching bracelets, with Alyssa at Heather's home in London.

Alyssa helps Loretta put on her earrings.

Wally helped Loretta put on her liners for four years
before she could manage them by herself.

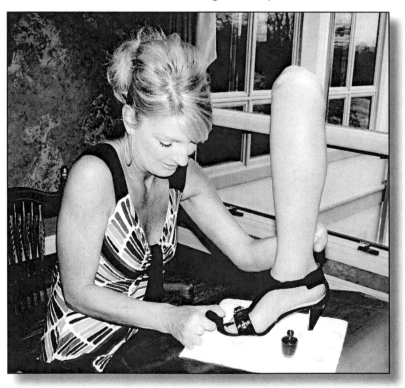

Loretta painting her toenails.

Bruno, Dr. Pillet's technician, paints Loretta's
prosthetic hand to match her skin.

Loretta with Dr. Jean Pillet, the hand prosthetist from
Paris, who used a mold of Loretta's arm to make a prosthetic glove.

Loretta puts on her prosthetic hand.

Mirka Figueroa, owner of Dutch Hollow Medical Spa,
rubs lotion on Loretta's arm.

Loretta and Lisa Feuerbach.

Loretta and fellow
amputee,
Dave Diestelhorst, after a
garage sale blanket brought
them together.

Loretta with Nurse Steve—her hair had grown out
and his ponytail had been cut.

Wally's sister, Nancy, urged Loretta to try new things, like starting the car.

202

Loretta's parents, Charles and Wanda Keck.

The Keck girls (from left): Linda, Loretta, Wanda, Laura, and Lola.

The Goebel family—Alyssa, Wally, Loretta, and Mitch—two years
after they moved to Edwardsville.

Loretta in the Rough.

Afterwords

Loretta sums it up

If I had been told that I would lose my limbs, I would have said, "There is no way I can get through that. And even if I did, I wouldn't want to live!"

But standing on this side of the equation, I realize that is not true. God places certain people in your life when you need them most. People who help you through the rough patches. People who will love you, no matter what. People who will catch and care for your family when you can't. People who will pray for you and believe in you when you have lost faith in yourself.

It is because of all those beautiful souls who were placed in my life that I survived, grew strong, and went on with my life. I thank God for every one of them. Their faith, prayers, and loving support, along with God's grace, made me the "miracle" I am today.

I also thank the loving souls that God continues to place in my life. These are people who only know me as I am today. Without all of them, my life would be without sunshine and normalcy. I thank them for "not knowing" until I told them.

It took time to find the true me again in the mirror. But eventually, I found her. I can't imagine what my life would be like now if I had decided to let the amputations beat me and keep me at home and uninvolved in life. I would have missed so much with my children, my family, old friends, the people who I've tried to help through example, and the myriad of new friends I've made.

I met Vicki Bennington, one of the authors of this book, in October 2005. All she knew ahead of time was that she was going to write an article about a woman who was a multiple amputee and was scheduled to speak at Dutch Hollow Medical Spa.

I arrived that afternoon full of excitement to be featured in the newspaper, and when I first walked in, I was confident that she wouldn't have a clue that I was the one she was going to interview. My motto has been, "If you didn't know my story, you wouldn't know my loss." And it worked that afternoon. When she saw me, she was puzzled. I was not what she expected. The element of surprise was fun.

Vicki asked me a multitude of questions, but took barely a note. After photos, tears, and conversation, we parted ways. When the story came out in print, I read it aloud to my children and cried. Vicki had touched my heart with her words—and I even knew the story up close and personal.

A couple of years later, she called to ask me if I would be open to something new. She and Daniel Brannan wanted to write my story in book form.

Flattered? You bet. God had allowed me to live for a purpose, and if the two of them were going to be his tools in getting my story into the hands and hearts of those who I could help or inspire, then I was delighted to be a part of such a project. I told her there was no one I would rather have do it.

Vicki and Dan interviewed me, as well as a lot of the key people who were in our lives at the time of my illness. We met over coffee, lunch, evenings around the table, and the three of us spent hours and hours in the public library. It has been a healing process to relive each and every step in this huge chapter of my life.

As God would have it, Vicki and Dan allowed me to be "Loretta in the Rough," cried with me, and have not only become business partners in a book adventure that I pray will help others to overcome and to find inner strength and peace in their life, but also friends who have touched me by their love for me and my family, and support me in my passion to be someone else's "Heather" in whatever crises they face.

God places people in your life that you need and that will enhance your world. Vicki and Dan helped me to put into words my struggles, feelings, fears, strengths, and faith. When Nancy Baumann of Stonebrook Publishing first read the manuscript, she told us that if she hadn't found it worthwhile, she would not have accepted the project, but she saw the hope my story would give people and was anxious to be part of it. She, too, has become as much a friend as business partner, and I thank God for placing her in my life, as well.

My doctor told me that ninety percent of patients who have toxic shock syndrome as severe as I had it, die. I believe I survived because of God's plan for me, and I believe that all of you are part of that plan. So what exactly is the plan? Good question, because I ponder that myself. Only God knows, but there are a few things I hope everyone keeps in mind long after they close the cover of this book:

- There is power in prayer.

- The importance of faith, family, and friends.

- Taking care of yourself should be No. 1 (the best "you" allows you to give your best to others).

- To be thankful every day for that day.

- That you can "re-bloom," no matter what happens.

- That if you look hard enough, you will see the silver lining in every dark cloud.

- Life truly is "one step at a time."

- It is okay to allow others to help you.

- That "parts is parts." It is what's inside that counts.

- That we are not to know the future. Leave it to God, because if I had known my fate, I might have decided that I would rather die than face it—and I would have missed so much.

Heartfelt Thanks

There are so many people that I want to thank, it seems almost daunting. How do I thank God for the gift of life, and for giving me the stubbornness to fight for it? Words alone are not enough.

From the bottom of my heart, I also thank:

- All my family members, for my parents for raising me in a home of love, faith, and prayer; giving me strength, tending to me and my family with The Changing of the Grandmas when we needed you most; to each and every one of my sisters; Linda for being by my side and praying fervently for my survival, and her husband, Buddy, who supported her through all of it; Laura for prayers, chats, placing the cross on my arm, countless weekends she came up to help me, and raising me up to sit on the barstools; her husband, Brian, who held down the fort at home; Lola who prayed and had faith that I would survive, keeping order in my home with all of the family there, and her husband, Brian, for safely and quickly getting my sisters to my bedside. Penny Laws, my mother-in-law, for always loving me as a daughter and caring for all of my needs through The Changing of the Grandmas; her husband, Fred, for jumping right in wherever we needed him and for addressing all of our thank you notes, and for his homemade hash browns. Diane, my sister-in-law for being a sister to me and helping to educate the family with her medical knowledge. My sister-in-law, Nancy, for many laughs, cheering, helping me to compromise or fix things to be "Loretta-friendly," for all of her love and being "Aunt Nancy" for Mitch and Alyssa as we traveled for new legs and hands, for dedicating love and time to our family. And thanks to all of our extended family for their prayers and support and the many ways they helped.

- Nurse Steve, whose medical knowledge helped save my life, and whose kindness and compassion comforted me during my illness.

- All the medical staff that went outside the norm to make me feel better with special lotions, early baths to feel fresh, gription tape for my water, allowing me to wear my own pjs, letting me cry with physical and emotional pain.

- Heather Mills for being my "angel" and taking the time to help and support me and for gracing this book with her own words.

- Bob and Tessa Watts, David Hills, and the whole crew at Dorset Orthopaedic who did everything they could to make me feel comfortable and did a wonderful job in all aspects of the construction of my new glamour legs.

- Dr. Jean Pillet and his prosthetist, Bruno, who fashioned a beautiful hand that makes me happy.

- Dick Snyder and Margie Barnes, whose wonderful pictures captured the way I felt.

- The entire community of Sycamore that caught my family as it fell into a dire time of need. As a group–and individually–they prayed for us, supported us, and embraced us.

- My church family, who held a cake auction and prayed for a miracle that came true, and our church group who were always there for us.

- Greg and Vicki Schoof for the love of our family and support of Wally, and all of Wally's work friends who held a fundraiser for medical bills and supported him through the ups and downs of my illness and recovery process.

- Lisa Feuerbach, who is like a sister to me, thanks for the prayers, song, and gift of music, and for not giving in to what the doctor said, but maintaining faith in God. Thank you for requesting a Bible and listening to the Holy Spirit, following your heart as you read to me and prayed for me; for the prayer vigil and community involvement on behalf of me and mine.

- Ann Thompson, who wrote the initial email to Heather Mills that changed my entire outlook for recovery and coping with my losses, and who, along with Amy Ridenour, helped me to look like "Mom" for myself and my family.

- Gracia Polarek for the many train rides to see my doctors and prosthetist in Chicago, laughing and talking, making me feel like we were on a holiday instead of a mission to do something that, of course, I would rather not have had to do.

- Neighbors for the Christmas lights, helping hands, love, prayers, and support when and wherever needed.

- Carolyn Reifsteck at the hospital and at home, for helping to find things that were "Loretta-friendly," for the bracelets, and also for being a fabulous neighbor and best friend.

- Mary Phelan, who saw the need of a girlfriend and acted on it. Thanks for being my friend and believing in my recovery; knowing I had given a "thumbs up" and would survive; for your prayers, support, shoulder, and endless tears we shared together; for all your travels from Ohio to see me; encouraging words and keeping my spirits up.

- Fred and Lisa Dewitt for being such good Christian friends. Lisa—for your prayers and love for our family. Fred—for your concern about possible stretch marks when they were treating me that you knew I wouldn't like; and for finding humor for Wally and taking him away from the hospital for lunch.

- Kathy Hammes for the inspirational blanket and for thinking of me when she saw it. It ultimately became the gift that kept on giving.

- Mirka Figueroa for recognizing that my story was a gift to share with others, and for giving me the platform to do so for the very first time.

- Mary Lee for taking over dance mom duties for me, so that the Grandmas would not have to do so much running. Thanks for crying for me.

- All those who wrote, sent cards and letters, sent emails, said prayers, etc., etc., etc., many whom I will never know—I thank wholeheartedly for caring for and raising the hopes of a stranger.

- And most of all, I thank Wally, Mitch, and Alyssa for being there for me through all the ups and downs. I'm thankful to Wally for remaining in research mode, always trying to find what was best for me; seeking a second opinion; being my eyes and ears when I needed him to be, all the while keeping the household running, working his job and making sure Mitch and Alyssa were taken care of. Mitch and Alyssa had to grow up quick, and even though we tried not to change their day-in and day-out routine, change was inevitable.

If I have forgotten to mention anyone, it's only a momentary lapse. I remember, appreciate, and know I benefited from every single person that touched my life during and after my illness—all who took time from their own busy lives to pray for me and my family; who said or displayed a single act of kindness or compassion—thank you so much!

Loretta

Vicki Bennington

I first met Loretta when I wrote a feature article about her experience and amazing recovery. When she walked into the room I couldn't comprehend that she had multiple amputations. She looked perfectly fit and far from devastated.

As she told her story, my heart melted for her, we cried together, but I could see she hadn't let it stop her from living. And through the process of writing this book, talking to her about *everything*—she has become a very close and dear friend who I hope will remain in my life. She's truly a wonderful person.

I want to thank Loretta for sharing her story with me, and allowing Daniel Brannan and I to help her share it with everyone else, and I am thankful for Dan through the long and arduous process. I would like to thank our publisher, Nancy Baumann, who saw the value in the story, and became just as big a fan of Loretta's as the rest of us. Her pushing and prodding to expand, embellish, and persevere helped us bring Loretta's personality to the written page. Richard Snyder, an outstanding photographer, volunteered his services to stage several photo shoots to provide beautiful pictures for the book.

I also thank Heather Mills for graciously writing the foreword, and Renata Matijasevic and Sonya Mills for helping me along the way. Bob and Tessa Watts at Dorset Orthopaedic kindly shared their knowledge and provided a personal tour of the factory where Loretta's and Heather's glamour legs were made, which was an invaluable learning experience. There were many others, including our families, who helped guide our paths to the completion of this long journey, and I am so grateful for all of them.

Daniel Brannan

I first met Loretta Goebel in spring 2007, after *The Telegraph* in Alton, Illinois, published an in-depth story about her. The more I learned about what Loretta had to overcome to get back on her feet, the more in awe I became of her.

I am insulin dependent and have worried that, one day, I might have problems with my own extremities. Many diabetics eventually have one or more of their limbs amputated, and Loretta has given me hope that such a situation would not result in disaster.

I thank Nancy Baumann of Stonebrook Publishing for her editing and encouragement through the process. I am also thankful for my friendship with Loretta and Vicki. I think the three of us make quite a team. A special thanks to Heather Mills for her help with the project and her support of Loretta. I don't know if Loretta could have made it through some of her most difficult times without Heather's helping hand.

Book Club Study Questions

1. Loretta and Wally's marriage suffered and died as they coped with the trauma thrust upon them. How does tragedy affect a marriage? How do you think your own relationships would have changed if you were Loretta? If you were Wally? What do you think happened to them?

2. Imagine what your life would be like if you lost one hand entirely and had only a thumb and a partial forefinger on the other. Try doing the simple things Loretta described, like starting the car, making a sandwich, setting the table, or getting dressed. How would you have to adapt to cope with this lifestyle?

3. Think about Loretta's parents, Charles and Wanda. What would it be like to watch your child suffer through a near-death experience followed by systematic amputations? What emotions would you experience? How would you deal with them?

4. What was it about Loretta that didn't allow her to indulge in self-pity? Was it part of her personality, or was it borne of practice? What causes people to wallow in their circumstances? How can Loretta's story change your own attitude about the problems you face?

5. What role do you think diet, exercise, and a healthy lifestyle played in Loretta's recovery? Why was she so determined to push herself to exercise? How does her example crush excuses for not taking care of your own body?

6. Try getting around on your knees like Loretta did for one hour. How does your perspective change? What did you learn? What would your life be like without your lower legs?

7. Loretta's experience with Heather Mills allowed her to see Heather in a different light from how the media portrayed her. Did you know anything about Heather before reading the book? Did your opinion of her change? How do you think media attention—positive or negative—molds public opinion? What lessons can you draw from Loretta's experience with Heather?

8. Loretta had to depend on her children to survive. How do you think this type of role-reversal affects children? How might it mold their personalities? Their character? What, if any, permanent changes might take place in the parent-child relationship?

9. Why doesn't Loretta want others to know she's an amputee? What lengths did she go to in order to be seen as "normal?" How would you want to be perceived?

10. Imagine yourself as Loretta was before her amputations when her legs were black and her hands were useless. How would you feel about your body and the lack of self-sufficiency? How would your self-image be affected? How do you think other people would respond to you? Would your relationships change?

11. It is not uncommon for people to suffer amputations through complications of diabetes, through combat, or through accidents. What other life changes can feel like an amputation? How can Loretta's story inspire those who have both visible and "invisible" amputations? To those who must manage a disease or a disability? To those who have suffered other losses?

Appendix I: Strep Toxic Shock Syndrome

- Strep toxic shock syndrome is a serious, but uncommon, bacterial infection.

- The strep toxic shock incident rate in the United States was extremely rare at last count, approximately 1 in 4,449,016 or 0.001 percent.

- 90 percent of those with the type of strep toxic shock that Loretta Goebel suffered, die.

- The symptoms of strep toxic shock include sudden high fever, faintness, confusion, watery diarrhea, headache, and muscle aches. Another symptom is a red infection line emanating from the point of entrance.

- Limb loss from strep toxic shock depends on the situation. The loss of limbs is not from the strep itself, but lack of blood circulation to the extremities during treatment.

Source: Dr. Bernard C. Camins, associate professor of medicine, Washington University School of Medicine, St. Louis, Missouri

Appendix II: Resources for Amputees

Dorset Orthopaedic
Ringwood, Hants, in Dorset County, England
www.dorset-ortho.co.uk

The Amputee Coalition of America
www.amputee-coalition.org

Heather Mills
www.heathermills.org

The American Board for Certification in Orthotics & Prosthetics
www.abcop.org

Limbs for Life
www.limbsforlife.org

Hanger Prosthetics and Orthotics
www.hangar.com
(877) 4HANGER

Dr. Jean Pillet
www.pillet.com

In the United States:
(800) 331-HAND (4263)
email: info@pillet.com

In France:
01 47 42 55 23
email: contact@pillet.com

The Limbless Association, U.K.
www.limbless-association.org

Wiggle Your Toes, U.S.
www.wiggleyourtoes.org
(952) 221-0500

Orthotics and Prosthetics Edge
www.oandp.com

Loretta Goebel
www.lorettagoebel.com

This is a small sampling of literally hundreds of active organizations that can offer help or hope to amputees.

CPSIA information can be obtained at www.ICGtesting.com
Printed in the USA
LVOW13s1159310114

371801LV00003B/6/P